Reflections on Elizabeth A. H. Green's Life and Career in Music Education

T0299855

An engaging integration of scholarship and storytelling, *Reflections on Elizabeth A. H. Green's Life and Career in Music Education* details the life and career of a pioneering figure in the field of instrumental music teacher education, who was one of the first to document a curriculum for teaching conducting and stringed instruments. Featuring interviews with Green's former students, faculty colleagues, and close friends, this account combines reflections and memories with Green's conducting techniques and teachings. *Reflections on Elizabeth A. H. Green's Life and Career in Music Education* uncovers pedagogical insights not available in the late educator's published texts, focusing on ways to assist instructors in new and different ways to manage and direct large ensembles and build confidence in undergraduate music majors. Through the exploration of an extraordinary educator's life, it offers new insights into both the history of music education and present-day pedagogy for string instruments and conducting.

Jared R. Rawlings is Associate Professor of Music Education and Associate Director of the School of Music at the University of Utah.

Reflections on Elizabeth A. H. Green's Life and Career in Music Education

Jared R. Rawlings

Routledge
Taylor & Francis Group

NEW YORK AND LONDON

First published 2022
by Routledge
605 Third Avenue, New York, NY 10158

and by Routledge
4 Park Square, Milton Park, Abingdon, Oxon, OX14 4RN

Routledge is an imprint of the Taylor & Francis Group, an informa business

Library of Congress Cataloging-in-Publication Data
Names: Rawlings, Jared, author.
Title: Reflections on Elizabeth A. H. Green's life and career in
music education / Jared R. Rawlings.
Description: New York: Routledge, 2022. |
Includes bibliographical references and index.
Identifiers: LCCN 2021053460 (print) | LCCN 2021053461 (ebook) |
ISBN 9780367715151 (hardback) | ISBN 9780367715168 (paperback) |
ISBN 9781003152415 (ebook)
Subjects: LCSH: Green, Elizabeth A. H. |
Music teachers–United States–Biography. |
Stringed instruments–Instruction and study–United States–
History–20th century. | Conducting–Instruction and study–
United States–History–20th century.
Classification: LCC ML423.G776 R38 2022 (print) |
LCC ML423.G776 (ebook) | DDC 780.71 [B]–dc23
LC record available at https://lccn.loc.gov/2021053460
LC ebook record available at https://lccn.loc.gov/2021053461

ISBN: 978-0-367-71515-1 (hbk)
ISBN: 978-0-367-71516-8 (pbk)
ISBN: 978-1-003-15241-5 (ebk)

DOI: 10.4324/9781003152415

Typeset in Times New Roman
by Newgen Publishing UK

Contents

Figures

Foreword

Elizabeth Green was the greatest teacher I ever had of anything. It was my good fortune to have Professor Green as my conducting teacher when I first arrived as a student at the University of Michigan in the early 1950s. Immediately, I knew I was in the presence of greatness, with someone who cared deeply for all her students (including me). I learned not only about conducting, and later string instrument technique, from a master teacher, but also how to teach just by observing how she taught. What meaningful lessons I learned about conducting, string instruments, teaching, and life!

When I returned to the University of Michigan as a faculty member in 1975, I would spend time on many occasions just talking with her in her home. During one of these visits, I noticed her old TV with a "rabbit ears" antenna. In addition, it had rubber bands attached to the dials. Upon asking her the purpose of the rubber bands, she said that if she put pressure on the dials, the stations would come in more clearly. I made note of that, and when I returned to my home, I called six or eight of my friends who had been her students and asked for $100 each to buy her a new TV (with cable). I could have asked many, many more of her former students – such was the respect, admiration, and love we all felt for her.

Her classes were essential, for we all learned so very much; we didn't want to miss anything. We were learning the grammar of conducting. This was during a time when she was also conducting her own junior high school orchestra in Ann Arbor. We were then lucky enough to be able to attend her own rehearsals and witness how it was really done.

Dr. Jared Rawlings' book will be treasured by the many students and friends of Elizabeth Green for it has been researched so very well and filled with the details of her life. It also includes personal reflections by a number of her former students. In this book, Dr. Rawlings details the life and achievements of Professor Green so completely that I, who knew her quite well, learned many aspects of her life and teaching that were unknown to me. He did not leave out the personal side or her dedication to her students. In reading the book, you learn not only the trajectory of her achievements but also the love and care she gave to and received from her many, many students.

H. Robert Reynolds
Director Emeritus of University Bands
Arthur Thurnau Emeritus Professor of Music (Conducting)
University of Michigan

Preface

> The acquiring of knowledge is not the end; the end is the use to which
> the knowledge is put.
>
> –Elizabeth A. H. Green.

This book tells the story of Elizabeth A. H. Green's life and career in music education. Throughout this book, the term "music education" is used, intended to encompass her work within formal music learning settings (schools, churches). The majority of music education research related to instrumental music and conducting pedagogy demonstrates that teaching a large instrumental ensemble is complex work.[1] Traditions of ensemble performance permeate the discourse of music education, broadly, while contemporary tensions related to the demands and constraints of teaching and the process of musical learning contribute to the complexities of musical teaching. Within this context, the music education field can benefit from research that examines the past teachings of music pedagogues in order to assist in understanding why these complexities exist today and how influential instructors have grappled with them in the past.

This historical account is written for K–12 music teachers and college professors who are responsible for preparing future teachers for K–12 instrumental music classrooms. Extant research documenting the influence of early music teacher educators is scarce, and current trends in music education historical research reveal that studies of women music educators can uncover an alternative view of the history of music education.[2] Since women have been somewhat silenced in historical records, this book will complement histories already documented in music education and serve as an example for future research on women in music education.[3]

Elizabeth A. H. Green was an innovative music teacher educator who influenced thousands of music educators and teacher educators in the 20th century. There is much to learn from examining the life and careers of early music teacher educators. By drawing upon the memories and recollections of Elizabeth's former students, colleagues, friends, and her own writings, I uncovered some of the idiosyncrasies of Elizabeth Green's pedagogy as a means of possibly enhancing the understanding of our present pedagogy for string instruments and conducting courses within institutions of higher education. How do Elizabeth's friends and close acquaintances describe her life within the context of her career in music education? How do Elizabeth's former students and colleagues describe and reconstruct her teaching? To what extent, if any, did her approach to teaching shift when considering the content and methods of her courses? How do these participants describe the impact of her teaching and praxis on her students? Within a male-dominated music profession, how did Elizabeth navigate some of the vocation-specific micropolitics? Many of us – teachers, preservice teachers, teacher educators, educational researchers – may have never asked ourselves these questions about Elizabeth or other early music teacher educators. On the other hand, some may have asked these questions with few presuming certain answers to these questions.

Researching and writing this book did not resolve those questions for me. Readers may come to accept the likelihood that the answers can never be known with definite certainty. This is due to the colossally complex, widespread, profoundly personal, indisputably social, intrinsically political, and inevitably subjective nature of the outcomes of music teaching and learning. The process of searching for these answers led to more questions. Who was teaching music during Elizabeth's life? What backgrounds do these music educators come from? Where were they teaching, and what was the relationship between music teaching in schools and at home? How were music educators involved in professional music organizations? What was the cultural and political climate during Elizabeth's life?

The nature of this book was influenced by the research and developments in the fields of historical research and human inquiry. The book investigates the meaning of teacher–student relationships within the life narratives of those who lived and experienced Elizabeth's teaching and career in music education and also offers an analysis of the significance of those relationships from my own worldview as a music teacher educator and researcher. Many details of how this investigation was conducted are included within Appendix D.

An Overview of the Book

This book is divided into five parts. The first two parts comprise Elizabeth's biographical information. The final three parts are devoted to an exploration of what made Elizabeth A. H. Green a master pedagogue, and looks into her pedagogy and relational capacity. Here, in somewhat greater detail, is what awaits the reader of this book.

Chapter 1 presents biographical material related to Elizabeth Green's life and career in music education – her relocation from Waterloo, Iowa, to Ann Arbor, Michigan, as the concluding event. In the first section of the chapter, I present her family background as well as her early music and formal music education experiences. In the next section of the chapter, I discuss Green's public school teaching career and professional experiences in Waterloo, Iowa. Although my research includes referencing previously documented material, I was granted access to much personal information documented within holdings at historical libraries. Many of the pictures within this chapter exist in the Wheaton College Special Collections and East Waterloo High School Yearbooks.

Chapter 2 is a continuation of Elizabeth's biography. In the first section of the chapter, I present her teaching career in both secondary and tertiary education in Ann Arbor, Michigan. There are many details within this chapter that account for how Elizabeth navigated teaching for both Ann Arbor Public School District and the University of Michigan during her first decade living in Michigan. In the next section of the chapter, I detail the transition from part-time work to full-time work at the University of Michigan. Throughout this section of the chapter, I include artifacts detailing the courses she taught, her promotion through the ranks of higher education, and her retirement. Elizabeth was an extremely active professional – both teaching and performing. In the next section of the chapter, I document details of her professional activity while she was living in Ann Arbor. This includes her violin studies and performance career, professional conducting activities, professional studies with Nicoli Malko, guest teaching/speaking engagements, publications, and service to the music education profession. There are several photographs within this chapter, and they can be found in her paper collection at Bentley Historical Library (University of Michigan) and *Ann Arbor News* archives.

Based on these biographical details, Elizabeth's strong reputation as a leader in the fields of conducting and string performance makes her a unique figure in music education history. Within Chapter 3, I share selected quotes of interview data, assembled from her past students, friends, and colleagues, that relate to her pedagogy and teaching philosophy. In the first section of the chapter, I present Elizabeth's teaching philosophy as it relates to conducting and string pedagogy. Specifically, I discuss her strong-held, core beliefs about music and detail her commitment to content mastery and musicianship through experiential learning. In the second section of this chapter, I present how Elizabeth used her diagnostic skill as formative assessment toward a systematic way of learning and knowing. Elizabeth had a prominent reputation as a detailed diagnostician. From establishing her diagnosis, she was able to construct a prescriptive plan to address what needed to be corrected. In the final section of this chapter, I present evidence about how Elizabeth made clear her commitment to affective fulfillment and the use of imagination.

Chapter 4 presents information-rich descriptions of Elizabeth Green's tremendous capacity for building relationships with her students and colleagues throughout her life and career in music education. Notably, her *presence* in teaching music, which was profound, opens the chapter. Her persistence was a unique component to her teaching, and she could be persistent with her students through how she cultivated rapport and trust. Next, I present how Elizabeth created a *safe* learning space (physically and psychologically) that promotes learning. Within this chapter, I provide scholarly, interpretive frameworks for connecting and grounding the heartfelt narratives of her former students and friends.

The final chapter of this book, Chapter 5, is an exploration of a strong theme from the interviews. The title of the chapter, "Always Teaching," was a prominent point made by the interviewees. Elizabeth had a profound way of modeling the learning process as well as sharing what she had learned with her students and through her publications. I add a layer of ambiguity to the text, offering readers a pair of analytical lenses for viewing the phenomena presented in the earlier parts of the book. One tenet of her teaching philosophy was that teachers should encourage their students to be curious. Throughout this chapter, there is evidence of her teaching philosophy captured in the selected quotes. As such, a picture emerges of an array of musical outcomes that have been identified as significant by the interviewees, attributed to Elizabeth's influence, and situated within the complex network of ongoing life stories.

This book aims to promote a conversation between the story's readers, as each brings a distinctive perspective to the conversation. It is my hope that this book will lead to rich discussions about the purposes and meaning of music education and what can and should be accomplished in schools that might make a positive difference in the lives of youth. This book is an attempt to raise my own voice, not in an assertive fashion, but in one that entices readers to start such discussions. I believe that researching how a single music educator has taught, listening carefully to how her former students describe what they learned and appreciated over the decades, and thinking deeply about the significance of these memories (and what they fail to include) can give us much to discuss. This discussion may center around a need to document noteworthy educators and learn from their experiences, and in order to accomplish this work and understand the work of music teachers, researchers must continue to document experiences of those educators who may appear ordinary but led extraordinary lives and careers. As a result of this inquiry, profound ideas and questions may be raised about music teachers' *musical lives well lived.*

Notes

1 Sommer H. Forrester, "Music Teacher Knowledge: An Examination of the Intersections Between Instrumental Music Teaching and Conducting," Ph.D. diss., University of Michigan, Ann Arbor, 2015, ProQuest Dissertations and Theses Global (UMI No. 3731290).
2 Marie McCarthy, "Developments and Trends in Historical Research as Reflected in the *Journal of Historical Research in Music Education,* Volumes 21–30 (1999–2009)," *Journal of Historical Research in Music Education* 33, no. 2 (April 2012): 152–71.
3 Sondra Weiland Howe, *Women Music Educators in the United States: A History.* Scarecrow Press Inc., 2014.

Acknowledgments

This book has been years in the making. Along this journey investigating the career and life of Elizabeth A. H. Green, I have received assistance, inspiration, encouragement, and support from many people and institutions. I was inspired to start this investigation during my doctoral coursework at the University of Michigan (Ann Arbor, Michigan), and I especially want to acknowledge the help of Dr. Marie McCarthy (Professor of Music Education, University of Michigan). Without her encouragement and "bread crumbs," this investigation would have never been conceived. Her guidance, over the course of eight years, challenged my thinking, enhanced my writing, and supported the conception of this text. Onward!

I also want to thank the many contributors and interviewees; without their willingness to participate, the memories of Elizabeth may have been forgotten. These contributors were former students, colleagues, and friends of Elizabeth, and I extend deep appreciation and gratitude to the following:

E. Daniel Long
H. Robert Reynolds
Judith Palac
Barbara Barstow
Larry Livingston
Robert Jager
Larry Hurst
Paula Crider
Robert Phillips
Kevin Miller
Alice Sano
Joshua Feigelson
Louis Bergonzi

Janice Clark
Catherine Carignan
Michael Avsharian
Martha Froseth
Marijean Quigley-Young

There are other people who have contributed in important ways to completing this book. Two special people in my life served as readers for this book and I am so grateful for their thoughtful consideration and critique. Dr. Sommer Forrester and Dr. Shannan Hibbard, you will always be my *Ph.D. Pals*. Dr. Sommer Forrester and Dr. Molly Baugh served as external reviewers of my interview transcript analysis and support the validity of these quotes from the participants. Research assistant Dr. Seth Pendergast transcribed an enormous number of recorded interviews. Dr. Miguel Chuaqui and Dr. Mark Ely generously supported release time from teaching at a crucial point in the writing process, and the University of Utah, College of Fine Arts, provided funding for data collection and digitization of several of the photographs found within this book.

I am also grateful to several people at Routledge. Music Acquisitions Editor Constance Ditzel was willing to support a book based on historical research that sometimes oscillated between life history and oral history research and deviated from most texts written for professional educators. Editor Genevieve Akoi helped me in the final stages of production of this book and answered my many questions.

Finally, I have been blessed with the love of friends and family members. Thank you, Mom and Dad, Ally, Laura, and Brian. Without their constant encouragement, wisdom, and understanding, this book could not have been written.

1 Elizabeth A. H. Green (1906–1942)

*They were all ordinary until they took the extraordinary steps with courage
to leave the extraordinary footprints.*

– Ernest Agyemang Yeboah

After reading the Preface, it is clear that there is a need to document
noteworthy educators and learn from their teaching experiences.
Ostensibly, then, researchers must document experiences of those
music educators who may appear ordinary but led extraordinary lives
and careers in music education. In October 1951, a journal editor made
a statement about Elizabeth A. H. Green that expresses the feelings of
many of the informants captured within this book: "Where Elizabeth
Green finds the time for all the activities in her busy life is somewhat
of a mystery."[1]

This chapter presents a segment of biographical material related to
Elizabeth Green's life and career in music education – her relocation
from Waterloo, Iowa, to Ann Arbor, Michigan, as the concluding event.
In the first section of the chapter, I present her family background as
well as her early music and formal music education experiences. In the
next section of the chapter, I write about Green's public school teaching
career and professional experiences in Waterloo, Iowa.

Growing Up Musical (1906–1928)

Early Music Experiences

Elizabeth Adine Herkimer Green was born on August 21, 1906, in
Mobile, Alabama, to Albert Wingate Green and Mary Elizabeth
Timmerman. During her first two years of life, Elizabeth was
surrounded by the music-making of her parents.[2] As a professional

DOI: 10.4324/9781003152415-1

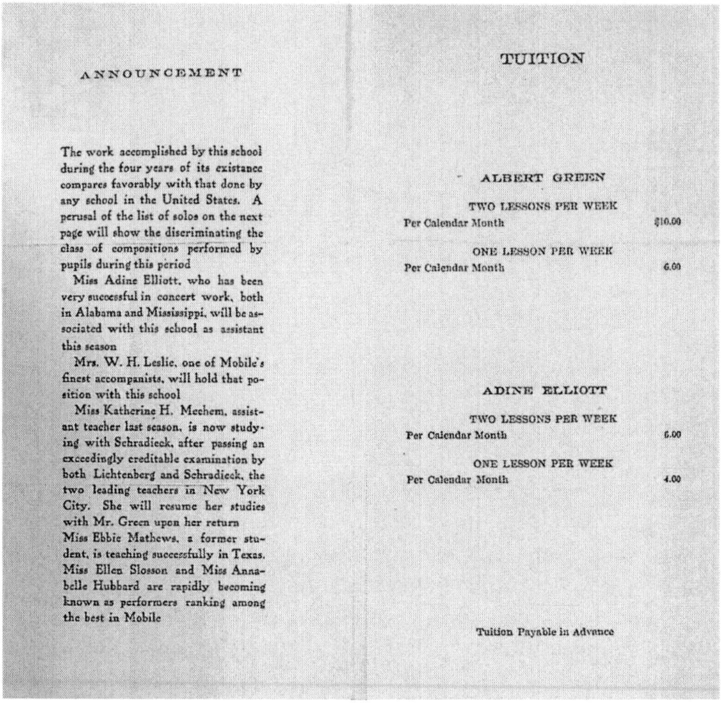

ANNOUNCEMENT

TUITION

The work accomplished by this school during the four years of its existance compares favorably with that done by any school in the United States. A perusal of the list of solos on the next page will show the discriminating the class of compositions performed by pupils during this period

Miss Adine Elliott, who has been very successful in concert work, both in Alabama and Mississippi, will be associated with this school as assistant this season

Mrs. W. H. Leslie, one of Mobile's finest accompanists, will hold that position with this school

Miss Katherine H. Mechem, assistant teacher last season, is now studying with Schradieck, after passing an exceedingly creditable examination by both Lichtenberg and Schradieck, the two leading teachers in New York City. She will resume her studies with Mr. Green upon her return

Miss Ebbie Mathews, a former student, is teaching successfully in Texas. Miss Ellen Slosson and Miss Annabelle Hubbard are rapidly becoming known as performers ranking among the best in Mobile

ALBERT GREEN

TWO LESSONS PER WEEK
Per Calendar Month $10.00

ONE LESSON PER WEEK
Per Calendar Month 6.00

ADINE ELLIOTT

TWO LESSONS PER WEEK
Per Calendar Month 6.00

ONE LESSON PER WEEK
Per Calendar Month 4.00

Tuition Payable in Advance

Figure 1.1 Albert Wingate Green *Violin School* Brochure, 52 South Jackson Street, Mobile, Alabama, circa 1906.

Source: Elizabeth Green Papers (SC-32), Buswell Library Special Collections, Wheaton, Illinois.

musician and violinist, and as founder of the *Mobile Violin School* (Figure 1.1), Albert Green was immersed in serving his community through teaching and refurbishing violins. Elizabeth vaguely remembered her father practicing violin, and occasionally he would give private lessons to children within their family home.[3] Within another memory, she also remembered hearing her mother, a retired nurse, playing short songs on their household piano.[4] Elizabeth recalled multiple memories of her father developing her hearing for music study, as he nurtured her music ability at an early age. She remarked that she would "cry on pitch," or matching the pitch, following her father playing a pitch on the piano.[5]

In 1908, the Green family moved from Mobile, Alabama, to Blue Island, Illinois, so Albert Green could assume the role of Director of the Violin Department of Ferry Hall at Lake Forest University.[6] At

2 years old, Elizabeth recalled her father intentionally cultivating her musical growth, and he noticed her curiosity in playing violin. It is not a surprise that Elizabeth began violin lessons at age 4, as she remarked that she was "sort of born with a fiddle bow in one hand."[7] Elizabeth began playing violin in third position, as her arms were too short to comfortably reach first position at the end of the neck of the instrument, and her first lessons focused on the fundamentals of tone production, including instrument position, posture, drawing the bow evenly from the frog to the tip of the bow, and left-hand finger placement.[8] She continued playing violin, and at the age of 5 years old, started giving public performances. Curiously, Elizabeth remembered not having anxiety or nervous feelings during these performances, and she attributes this to her parents not pressuring her to perform.

Early Formal Music Instruction

During Elizabeth's primary school education, the Greens moved from Blue Island to Chicago and resided at 5417 Cottage Grove Avenue (Chicago, Illinois, 60615).[9] While attending primary school, she received daily music classes that included rote singing, keeping a steady pulse, and reading music notation.[10] Elizabeth valued performing, and she performed solo repertoire for violin regularly during her childhood.[11] At this point in her life, Elizabeth's father, Albert, was Director of the Chicago Technical Violin School (Figure 1.3) and taught individual violin lessons at the Cosmopolitan School of Music and Dramatic Art (Figure 1.4) and the Conservatory of Chicago (Figure 1.5). Albert continued these positions until he received an invitation to join the faculty at Wheaton College.

Elizabeth and her mother spent the spring and summer of 1918 in Little Falls, New York, with Ella V. Timmerman, M.D., who was Mary Green's sister. During this time, Elizabeth attended a small, one-room schoolhouse near Little Falls so that she could complete her sixth-grade schooling.[12] Emma Timmerman[13] was Elizabeth's teacher and only taught one or two students enrolled in each grade, which allowed for much individualized instruction.[14] Not only did Elizabeth complete her sixth-grade education, but under the instruction of her teacher, she excelled and completed the seventh grade at District No. 8 (Manheim, New York; Herkimer County).[15] Elizabeth and her mother returned to Chicago in the late summer months; the reason or motivation for their stay in New York remains a mystery, although it is possible that the economic impacts of World War I required the relocation. During this time, Albert lost many of his private students to the American armed forces, leading to a decline in income.[16]

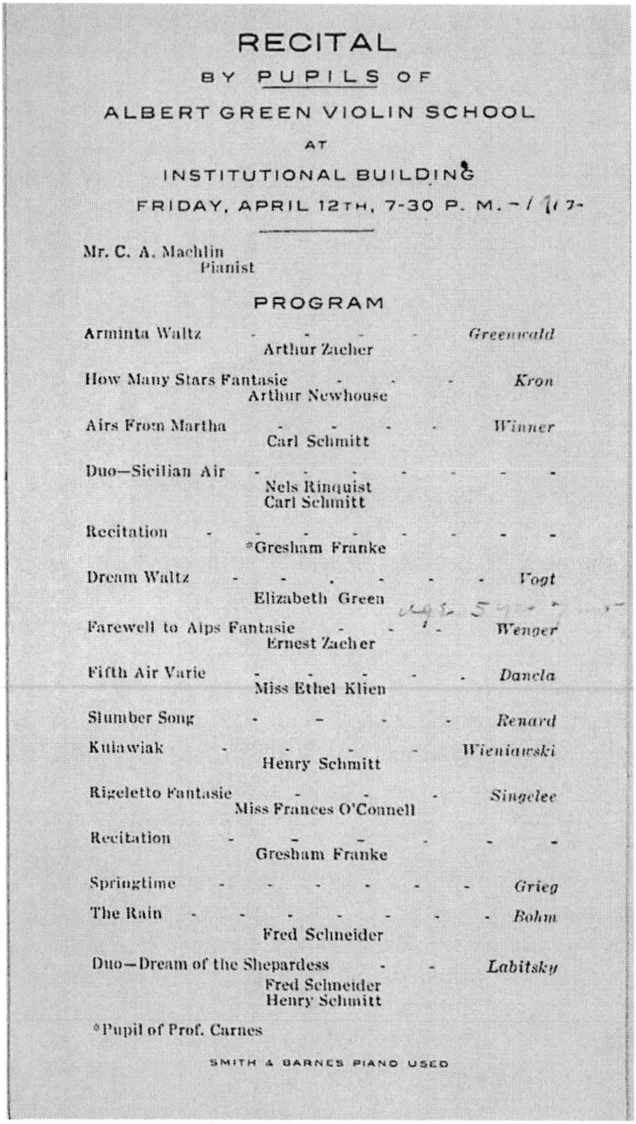

RECITAL

BY PUPILS OF

ALBERT GREEN VIOLIN SCHOOL

AT

INSTITUTIONAL BUILDING

FRIDAY, APRIL 12TH, 7-30 P. M.

Mr. C. A. Machlin
    Pianist

PROGRAM

Arminta Waltz	*Greenwald*
Arthur Zacher	
How Many Stars Fantasie	*Kron*
Arthur Newhouse	
Airs From Martha	*Winner*
Carl Schmitt	
Duo—Sicilian Air	
Nels Rinquist	
Carl Schmitt	
Recitation	
*Gresham Franke	
Dream Waltz	*Vogt*
Elizabeth Green	
Farewell to Alps Fantasie	*Wenger*
Ernest Zacher	
Fifth Air Varie	*Dancla*
Miss Ethel Klien	
Slumber Song	*Renard*
Kujawiak	*Wieniawski*
Henry Schmitt	
Rigeletto Fantasie	*Singelee*
Miss Frances O'Connell	
Recitation	
Gresham Franke	
Springtime	*Grieg*
The Rain	*Bohm*
Fred Schneider	
Duo—Dream of the Shepardess	*Labitsky*
Fred Schneider	
Henry Schmitt	

*Pupil of Prof. Carnes

SMITH & BARNES PIANO USED

Figure 1.2   Recital Program from April 12, 1912, Elizabeth Green performs *Dream Waltz* at age 5.

Source: Elizabeth Green Papers (SC-32), Buswell Library Special Collections, Wheaton, Illinois.

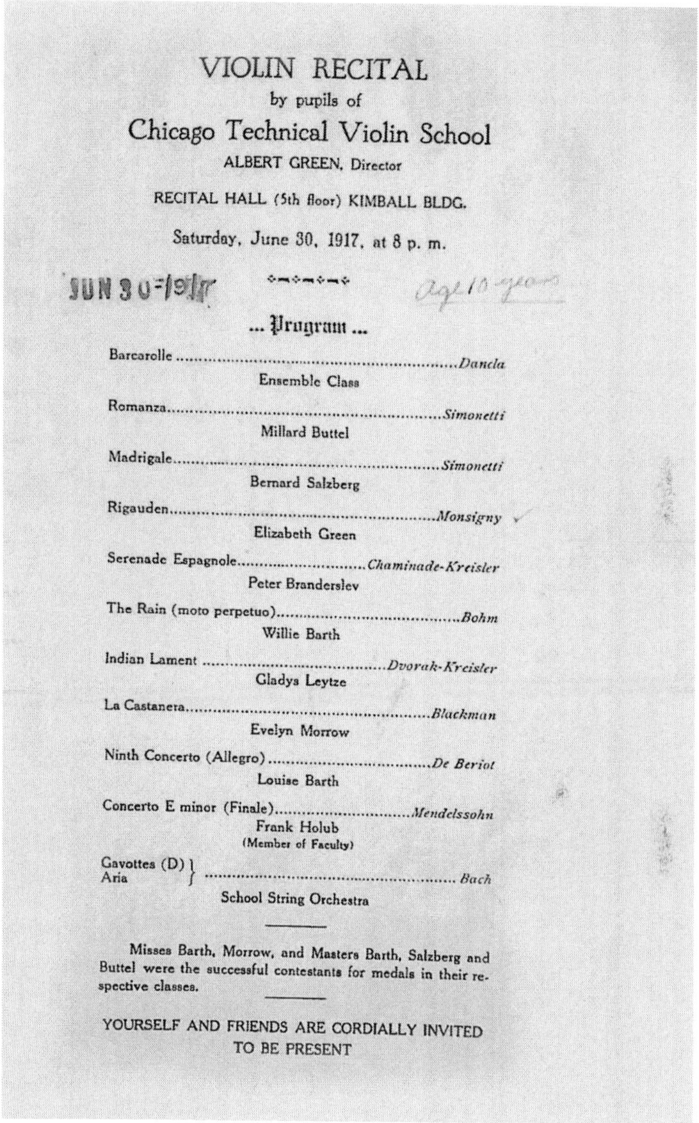

VIOLIN RECITAL
by pupils of
Chicago Technical Violin School
ALBERT GREEN, Director

RECITAL HALL (5th floor) KIMBALL BLDG.

Saturday, June 30, 1917, at 8 p. m.

JUN 30 1917 Age 10 years

... Program ...

Barcarolle .... *Dancla*
Ensemble Class

Romanza .... *Simonetti*
Millard Buttel

Madrigale .... *Simonetti*
Bernard Salzberg

Rigauden .... *Monsigny*
Elizabeth Green

Serenade Espagnole .... *Chaminade-Kreisler*
Peter Brandersley

The Rain (moto perpetuo) .... *Bohm*
Willie Barth

Indian Lament .... *Dvorak-Kreisler*
Gladys Leytze

La Castanera .... *Blackman*
Evelyn Morrow

Ninth Concerto (Allegro) .... *De Beriot*
Louise Barth

Concerto E minor (Finale) .... *Mendelssohn*
Frank Holub
(Member of Faculty)

Gavottes (D) }
Aria } .... *Bach*
School String Orchestra

Misses Barth, Morrow, and Masters Barth, Salzberg and Buttel were the successful contestants for medals in their respective classes.

YOURSELF AND FRIENDS ARE CORDIALLY INVITED
TO BE PRESENT

Figure 1.3 Recital Program from June 30, 1917, Elizabeth Green performs *Rigauden* at Chicago Technical Violin School, age 10.

Source: Elizabeth Green Papers (SC-32), Buswell Library Special Collections, Wheaton, Illinois.

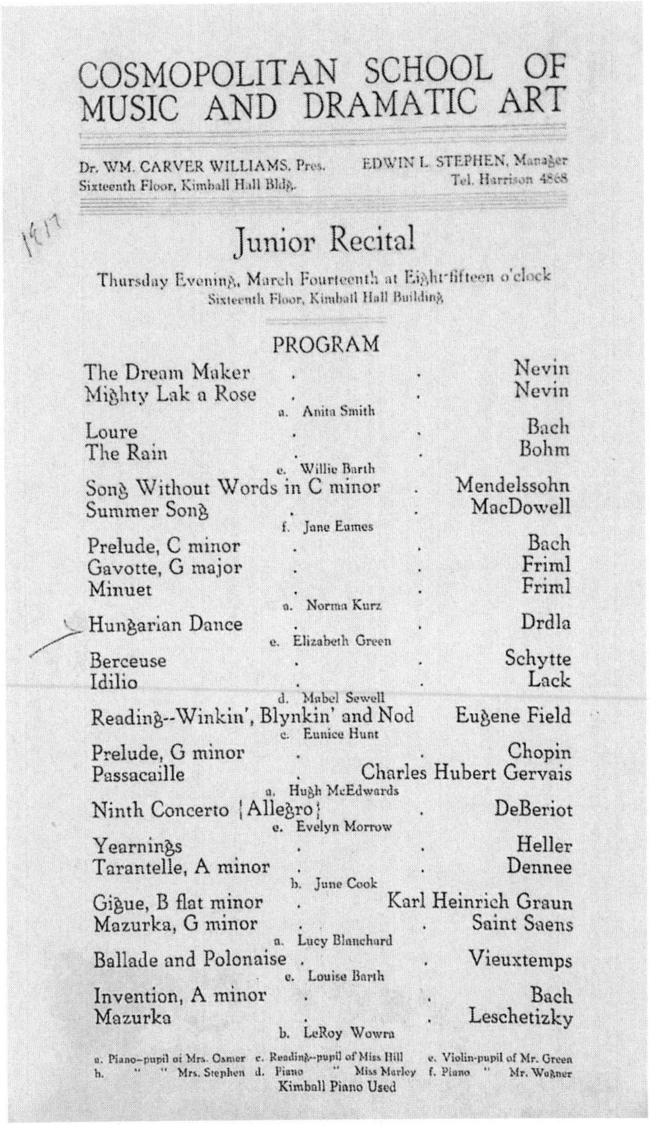

COSMOPOLITAN SCHOOL OF MUSIC AND DRAMATIC ART

Dr. WM. CARVER WILLIAMS, Pres.   EDWIN L. STEPHEN, Manager
Sixteenth Floor, Kimball Hall Bldg.   Tel. Harrison 4868

Junior Recital

Thursday Evening, March Fourteenth at Eight-fifteen o'clock
Sixteenth Floor, Kimball Hall Building

PROGRAM

The Dream Maker	Nevin
Mighty Lak a Rose	Nevin
a. Anita Smith	
Loure	Bach
The Rain	Bohm
e. Willie Barth	
Song Without Words in C minor	Mendelssohn
Summer Song	MacDowell
f. Jane Eames	
Prelude, C minor	Bach
Gavotte, G major	Friml
Minuet	Friml
a. Norma Kurz	
Hungarian Dance	Drdla
e. Elizabeth Green	
Berceuse	Schytte
Idilio	Lack
d. Mabel Sewell	
Reading--Winkin', Blynkin' and Nod	Eugene Field
c. Eunice Hunt	
Prelude, G minor	Chopin
Passacaille	Charles Hubert Gervais
a. Hugh McEdwards	
Ninth Concerto {Allegro}	DeBeriot
e. Evelyn Morrow	
Yearnings	Heller
Tarantelle, A minor	Dennee
b. June Cook	
Gigue, B flat minor	Karl Heinrich Graun
Mazurka, G minor	Saint Saens
a. Lucy Blanchard	
Ballade and Polonaise	Vieuxtemps
e. Louise Barth	
Invention, A minor	Bach
Mazurka	Leschetizky
b. LeRoy Wowra	

a. Piano--pupil of Mrs. Osmer   c. Reading--pupil of Miss Hill   e. Violin-pupil of Mr. Green
b.   "   "   Mrs. Stephen   d. Piano   "   Miss Marley   f. Piano "   Mr. Wagner
                        Kimball Piano Used

Figure 1.4 Recital Program from June 30, 1917, Elizabeth Green performs
Hungarian Dance at Cosmopolitan School of Music and Dramatic
Art, age 10.

Source: Elizabeth Green Papers (SC-32), Buswell Library Special Collections,
Wheaton, Illinois.

You are cordially invited to attend a
Recital by violin pupils of

Albert Green

in the Recital Room of

The Conservatory of Chicago

811 to 816 Lyon & Healy Building
64 East Jackson Boulevard

Saturday Evening, March 3, 1917

at eight o'clock

MAR 3.- 1917   *age—10 years*

PROGRAM

Ensemble class { Reverie - - - -	*Kennedy*
{ Easter morn (unaccompanied) - -	*Becker*
Dream waltz - - - - -	*Vogt*
Chester Hopps	
Rondo - - - - - -	*Beriot*
Millard Buttle	
Last Hope - - - - -	*Gottschalk*
Charles Caney - Miss Caney—Piano	
Sonear (Violin duet) - - - -	*Reichart*
Harold Kite - Bernard Salzberg - Miss Salzberg—Piano	
Angels dream - - - - -	*Lagne*
Leo Malkin	
Genius Loci - - - - -	*Thern*
Bernhard Salzberg	
Allegro (Concerto) - - - -	*Huber*
Arthur Zacher	
Menuet - - - -	*Porpora-Kreisler*
Elizabeth Green	
Gypsy Dance - - - -	*Ernst*
Willie Barth - Miss Barth—Piano	
Souvinir - - - - -	*Dridla*
Gladys Leitze	
Gypsy Dance - - - -	*Wi..*
Evelyn Morrow - Miss Morrow—Piano	
Adieux - - - - -	*Sarasat..*
Loiuse Barth	
Mrs. C. A. Miller—Accompanist	

Figure 1.5 Recital Program from June 30, 1917, Elizabeth Green performs
Menuet at the Conservatory of Chicago, age 10.

Source: Elizabeth Green Papers (SC-32), Buswell Library Special Collections,
Wheaton, Illinois.

During the summer of 1919, the Green family relocated to Wheaton, Illinois, where her father accepted a faculty position as Instructor of Violin and Orchestral Work at Wheaton College Music Conservatory.[17] The Conservatory of Music had been an established division of Wheaton College since its founding in 1860.[18] Albert Green was one of three full-time instructors in the Conservatory of Music, and during his first few years as a faculty member, Albert worked to extend the prominence of the Conservatory by developing their first degree program in music. According to the Wheaton College Bulletin in April 1919:

> In the Wheaton College Conservatory of Music, an effort is being made to develop a thoroughly modern and efficient conservatory which will be able to train those who wish to become professional musicians either as teachers or performers, as well as those who wish to study music as an accomplishment.[19]

Albert Green's commitment to advancing the Conservatory was fortified when he became the next Director of the Conservatory of Music.[20] In 1922, *The Tower*, Wheaton College's Yearbook, reported "Professor Green is spending his time untiringly in developing Wheaton's Conservatory and he has unquestionably strengthened it in every department."[21] Until Albert Green assumed the directorship of the Conservatory of Music, degrees in music had not been conferred by the college.[22]

During Elizabeth's secondary school education at Wheaton Academy and Wheaton High School, she was not challenged by the music curriculum. She sought out and was permitted to attend classes at the Music Conservatory at Wheaton College during her study breaks. She continued to study violin with her father and started completing the music requirements for a Bachelor of Music degree (Figure 1.6).[23]

Elizabeth was devoted to continuing her music studies, and when she graduated from Wheaton High School in 1924, she had also completed the Bachelor of Music degree requirements for Wheaton College. The music requirements included applied lessons (violin and cello), music ensemble participation, music theory and counterpoint, and music history.[24] Following her graduation from Wheaton High School, with only her general education requirements left to fulfill, Elizabeth pursued a Bachelor of Science degree, majoring in philosophy with minors in physics and French.[25] Elizabeth participated in the 1924 Wheaton College commencement exercises at the college; however, the degree with teaching licensure was not awarded until her general academic requirements were met in 1928.[26]

Figure 1.6 Elizabeth Green portrait, circa 1919.
Source: Elizabeth Green Papers (SC-32), Buswell Library Special Collections, Wheaton, Illinois.

Elizabeth was an accomplished violinist and after graduating from Wheaton High School, she was hired as an instructor of violin for the Wheaton Music Conservatory (Figure 1.7).[27] Uniquely, Elizabeth was both a student and faculty member at Wheaton College. Due to the increased enrollment of the Conservatory, Albert Green was in a position to hire additional faculty to accommodate the student population. Under the directorship of her father, Elizabeth was hired on as additional violin faculty member teaching only private violin lessons.[28]

Elizabeth performed dozens of recitals in and around the Chicago metropolitan area during the early 1920s, including concerts benefiting Wheaton College (Figure 1.8). An article printed in the *Wheaton Progressive* on May 25, 1923, expressed laudable reviews of Elizabeth's performance. One review stated: "Miss Green rendered one of her own

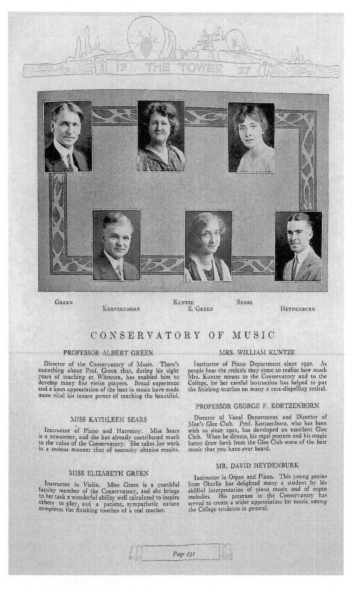

GREEN
KORTZENBORN
KUNTZE
E. GREEN
SEARS
HEYDENBURK

CONSERVATORY OF MUSIC

PROFESSOR ALBERT GREEN

Director of the Conservatory of Music. There's something about Prof. Green that, during his eight years of teaching at Wheaton, has enabled him to develop many fine violin players. Broad experience and a keen appreciation of the best in music have made more vital his innate power of teaching the beautiful.

MISS KATHLEEN SEARS

Instructor of Piano and Harmony. Miss Sears is a newcomer, and she has already contributed much to the value of the Conservatory. She takes her work in a serious manner that of necessity obtains results.

MISS ELIZABETH GREEN

Instructor in Violin. Miss Green is a youthful faculty member of the Conservatory, and she brings to her task a wonderful ability well calculated to inspire others to play, and a patient, sympathetic nature completes the finishing touches of a real teacher.

MRS. WILLIAM KUNTZE

Instructor of Piano Department since 1920. As people hear the recitals they come to realize how much Mrs. Kuntze means to the Conservatory and to the College, for her careful instruction has helped to put the finishing touches on many a care-dispelling recital.

PROFESSOR GEORGE F. KORTZENBORN

Director of Vocal Department and Director of Men's Glee Club. Prof. Kortzenborn, who has been with us since 1921, has developed an excellent Glee Club. When he directs, his regal posture and his magic baton draw forth from the Glee Club some of the best music that you have ever heard.

MR. DAVID HEYDENBURK

Instructor in Organ and Piano. This young genius from Oberlin has delighted many a student by his skillful interpretation of piano music and of organ melodies. His presence in the Conservatory has served to create a wider appreciation for music among the College students in general.

Page 151

Figure 1.7 Elizabeth Green, faculty member of the Conservatory of Music, Wheaton College, 1927–1928.

Source: Buswell Library Special Collections, Wheaton, Illinois.

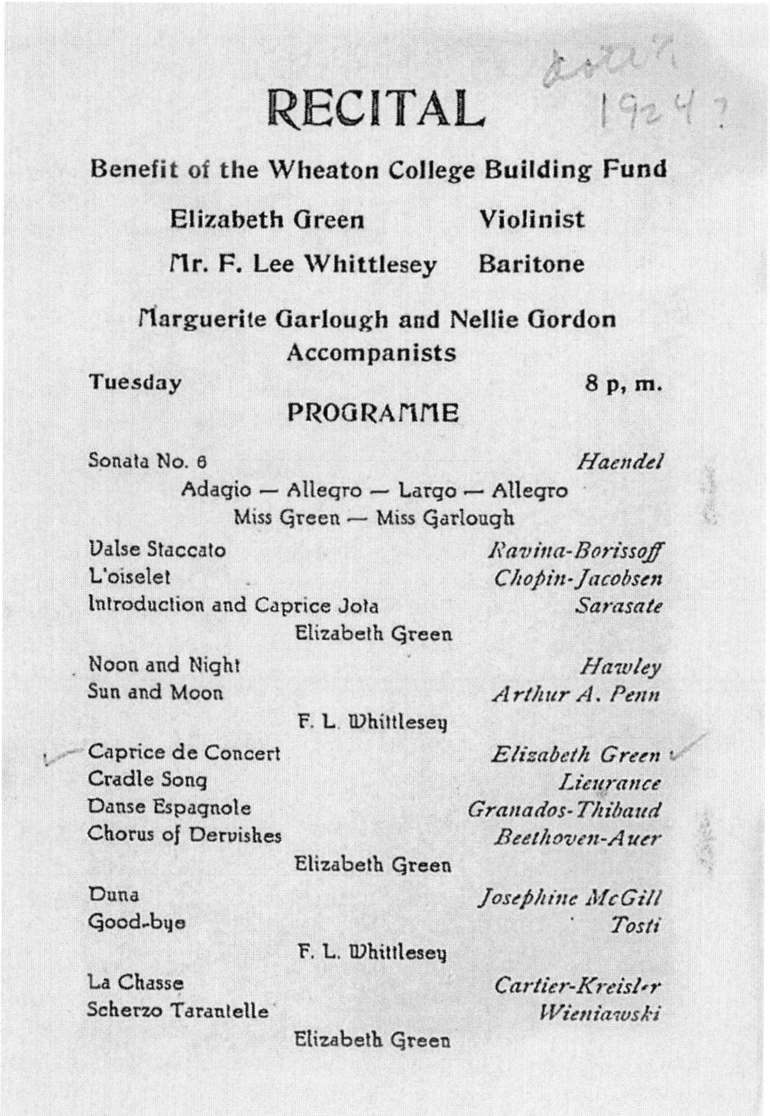

RECITAL

[handwritten: 1924 ?]

Benefit of the Wheaton College Building Fund

Elizabeth Green   **Violinist**

Mr. F. Lee Whittlesey   **Baritone**

Marguerite Garlough and Nellie Gordon
Accompanists

Tuesday   8 p. m.

PROGRAMME

Sonata No. 6   *Haendel*
    Adagio — Allegro — Largo — Allegro
        Miss Green — Miss Garlough

Valse Staccato   *Ravina-Borissoff*
L'oiselet   *Chopin-Jacobsen*
Introduction and Caprice Jota   *Sarasate*
                Elizabeth Green

Noon and Night   *Hawley*
Sun and Moon   *Arthur A. Penn*
                F. L. Whittlesey

Caprice de Concert   *Elizabeth Green*
Cradle Song   *Lieurance*
Danse Espagnole   *Granados-Thibaud*
Chorus of Dervishes   *Beethoven-Auer*
                Elizabeth Green

Duna   *Josephine McGill*
Good-bye   *Tosti*
                F. L. Whittlesey

La Chasse   *Cartier-Kreisler*
Scherzo Tarantelle   *Wieniawski*
                Elizabeth Green

Figure 1.8 Recital Program, circa 1924, Elizabeth Green performs at the Benefit of the Wheaton College Building Fund.

Source: Elizabeth Green Papers (SC-32), Buswell Library Special Collections, Wheaton, Illinois.

compositions [*Caprice de Concert*], which was very favorably received," and another reviewer wrote: "Miss Green was at her best, playing with skill and passion that the fine audience graciously accorded many pleasing encores."[29] One year later and at age 18, the *Wheaton College Record* printed a review of Elizabeth's solo violin performance.

> Miss Green's *Polonaise No. 1* was her most brilliant performance of the evening. *Bird as Prophet* showed great interpretive power, and *Chorus of Dervishes* imaginative qualities ... we wish that more of the students and town people could realize the real valued gained from these truly worth-while performances.[30]

In addition to performing concerts around the Chicago metropolitan area, she had other sources of income. Primarily, her faculty salary helped pay for her other studies at Wheaton College, where she was completing her general education requirements as well as another degree. Secondarily, Elizabeth was a grader for multiple courses across Wheaton College.[31] She earned not only a Bachelor of Music degree but also a Bachelor of Science degree with a major in philosophy, as well as receiving an Illinois teaching license.[32] After graduation, she declined a scholarship for graduate study at the University of Illinois and was offered two teaching positions – one at Morningside College in Sioux City, Iowa, and the other in East Waterloo Public Schools.[33] Elizabeth moved to East Waterloo to begin her public school teaching career, and Albert Green retired from active teaching in 1928.[34]

The Waterloo, Iowa Years (1928–1942)

East Waterloo Public Schools

Elizabeth relocated to Waterloo, Iowa, in the summer of 1928 and moved into a house occupied by two sisters located at 349 Vine Street (Waterloo, IA, 50703; across the street from the south side of East High School). At the beginning of the 1928–1929 school year, Elizabeth joined the faculty of East Waterloo Public Schools and assumed her assignment as an orchestra teacher at East High School. Primarily, Elizabeth was assigned to work alongside Grover Talmadge Bennett, who was Supervisor of Instrumental Music in East Waterloo and was primarily a wind, brass, and percussion instrument specialist.[35] With his large symphony orchestra of approximately 90 players, Elizabeth remembered:

> And that orchestra has every instrument that is needed for the largest scores and some kid trained to play it. We had E-flat flutes.

EAST SIDE HIGH AND MANUAL TRAINING SCHOOL, WATERLOO, IOWA.

Figure 1.9 East Waterloo High School, Waterloo, Iowa, circa 1930.
Source: Elizabeth Green Papers (SC-32), Buswell Library Special Collections, Wheaton, Illinois.

We had contra-bassoon and a heckelphone, which is a bass oboe. We had oboes and French horns, and of course we had an English horn. We even had a couple of sarrusophones, which are brass instruments played with a double reed, and two harps![36]

In addition to her teaching a school-based orchestra class at East Junior High and Senior High Schools, she was enthusiastic about teaching approximately 50 private violin and viola lessons each week – something she had been doing since she was 13 years old. One thing that challenged Elizabeth was that she had not formally studied viola prior to arriving in Waterloo, Iowa. Since she believed in the thought that "you can't teach what you don't know,"[37] Elizabeth taught herself the viola and was ready to start the school year.

The First Years of Teaching Public School Music and Private String Lessons

During her first year of teaching, Elizabeth wrote many letters each month to her parents, who were still living in Wheaton, Illinois. Taken altogether, it is clear from reading the correspondence that Elizabeth was very close with her parents and regarded their opinions highly.[38]

Figure 1.10 Top row left to right: Charlotte Atland (cello); Mary McNabb
(viola); Elizabeth Green (first violin); Margaret Miller (second
violin), circa 1932.

Source: Elizabeth Green Papers (SC-32), Buswell Library Special Collections,
Wheaton, Illinois.

She would routinely write to ask her father for his opinion about
sequencing violin etudes and repertoire for her students, and from
later letters, she adopted her father's recommendations. Moreover,
Elizabeth would inquire about her father's experiences with violin
repair and refurbishing, often asking him to send her a few instruments
for her more advanced students in Waterloo. In letters addressed to her
mother, Elizabeth would report her successes with sewing blouses or
dresses, including ink sketches of the patterns with ornate detail. On
rare occasions, she would include swatches of fabric within the letters
and boast about the low cost of material for her garment projects.

Most of the anecdotes within her letters described her teaching experiences, with both students and her colleagues. Accompanying these topics, Elizabeth would share with her parents some occasional personal information, including about her close friends alongside her experiences attending and performing at the local First Presbyterian Church.[39]

There were many remarkable experiences Elizabeth described in her letters to her parents. On one hand, these experiences included a successful induction as a faculty member in East Waterloo Public Schools, a thriving private lesson studio, and many opportunities to perform live on radio broadcasts (WJAM, Waterloo, IA). On the other hand, Elizabeth's first semester of teaching was not always successful. She mentioned in her October 31, 1928, letter to her parents that she struggled with her use of humor in the junior high orchestra class.

> Well, I got them all to laugh at themselves, and that's the first step in correcting a mistake publicly. Then I jumped on them individually at this Junior [High] Orchestra Rehearsal. We were having a great time, and even the impossible ones were getting long bows and nice wrists ... then I saw it and poor Sydney didn't have his bow on the edge at the frog. I reached over and turned it, saying, "Just a little more on the edge like this, Sydney." Well, I didn't think anything of that. I was calling everyone down. When we started the next piece, I looked at Sydney and the child was almost crying. He was just righting to keep back the tears ... it made me feel terrible to think I had hurt anyone so – especially, Sydney.[40]

The letter goes on to describe how she corrected her error, and by the end of the rehearsal, Sydney was smiling and was chosen as a "good example" or performance model by Elizabeth to demonstrate a passage of the repertoire.

Elizabeth took the advancement of her string students very seriously and left *no stone unturned* to make sure they had quality instruments to practice and perform on. There are many letters to her parents where Elizabeth alludes to wanting (herself or her father) to collect used violins to refurbish and sell them, at cost, to students who would need them. In late November 1928, she wrote that "most people don't want to put more than $30.00 into an instrument. You see, West Waterloo is full of cash. ... East Waterloo has very few who have money to spare."[41] Elizabeth took it upon herself to see to it that her students were playing on instruments that would produce characteristic tone and also motivate and build her students' confidence.[42]

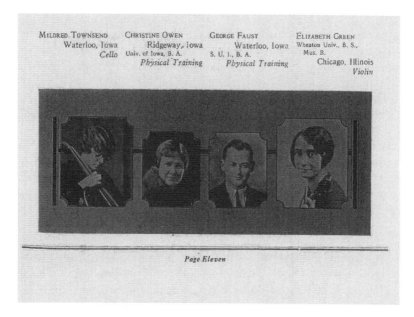

Figure 1.11 Elizabeth Green faculty portrait, East Waterloo High School
          Yearbook, 1929, page 11.
Source: Used with permission by Waterloo Public Schools.

During these first few years of teaching, Elizabeth made quite an impact on the Waterloo community and maintained a rigorous daily schedule. According to a letter on February 13, 1929, she documented her full teaching schedule to her parents; she started teaching at 8:00 a.m. with private lessons at the junior high school (approximately 14 students) and then taught school string ensemble rehearsals and lessons all afternoon and evening. Elizabeth's job included assisting Mr. Bennett in teaching all instrumental ensembles. Her duties included teaching 50 private lessons each week, as well as facilitating the senior high orchestra's string sectionals, which were held at 7:30 a.m. (before the start of the first class of the typical school schedule).[43] She reserved the evenings, sometimes until 10:00 p.m., for her own practicing and rehearsals as a performer.[44] She was a strong addition to the East instrumental music staff, especially in the area of private lessons and orchestra teaching.

The Second Stage of Teaching in Waterloo, IA[45]

In 1933, G. T. Bennett resigned from East High School to teach music at the college level,[46] and Elizabeth was appointed director of the orchestras

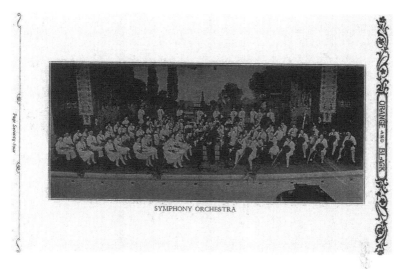

SYMPHONY ORCHESTRA

Figure 1.12 East Waterloo High School Symphony Orchestra, East Waterloo
High School Yearbook, 1929, page 68.
Source: Used with permission by Waterloo Public Schools.

at the junior and senior high schools.[47] Throughout Elizabeth's 14-year
tenure with East Waterloo Public Schools, she experienced the most
success teaching between 1935 and 1941. She led her music ensembles
to earn multiple accolades and laudable performances at both state and
national levels.

During this stage of her public school music teaching career,
Elizabeth's intellectual and musical curiosity developed in several ways.
As a dedicated string performer, she applied for and was accepted
to summer chamber music performance workshops and clinics. For
instance, Elizabeth was accepted to and attended the Gordon String
Quartet School[48,49] during the summer of 1931 in Falls Village,
Connecticut.[50] As an accomplished violinist and violist, Elizabeth was
counting on performing on both instruments during this experience;
however, in her acceptance letter, Clarence Evans[51] wrote:

> I should not advise you to practice Viola during your term with Mr.
> Gordon; I should recommend that you work like a beaver at the
> Violin, and make the very most of this wonderful chance that has
> been given you.[52]

Elizabeth worked diligently during the summer of 1931, and Jacques
Gordon invited her to return to the summer school in 1934, with a

ELIZABETH GREEN
Orchestra
*"Music is the universal language
and one in which she is well versed."*
Advisor of Music Committee of Friend-
ship Club.

Figure 1.13 Elizabeth Green faculty portrait, East Waterloo High School
Yearbook, 1934, page 15.
Source: Used with permission by Waterloo Public Schools.

third appearance in the summer of 1941 when she took three students,
including Larry Fisher.[53]

During this stage of her teaching career, Elizabeth was passionate
about string music teaching and wrote a number of articles for *The School
Musician.* A series of articles focused on qualified and fair adjudication
at music contests, most notably her article appearing in the January 1941
issue, entitled "The School Orchestra Stakes Out Its Claim." It elicited
a wide response, letters of both support and disapproval.[54] Elizabeth's
direct, narrative writing style throughout this article demands attention
from the reader and captures the author's urgency. Her controversial
message was simple in this article, centering around a string enrollment
crisis, where students were encouraged by multiple constituents to join
the marching band instead of string orchestra. The rivalry between
band and orchestra is explored in detail, and a new adjudication process for festivals is outlined and recommended. Another series on string
tone production appeared in 1936, which focused on how the Waterloo
Civic Symphony Orchestra applied the laws of physics to create a professional sound.[55]

Instrumental Music Adjudicated Events and Competitions

Instrumental music adjudicated events have been a topic of dialogue
among American music teachers since before the Great Depression,[56]
and the structure of Iowa's music competitions was a model for imita-
tion by other state activity associations.[57] Green's influence on the structure of Iowa's music competitions can be seen in several handwritten
letters addressed to her parents during the first few years of her teaching

in Waterloo, in which she documented details of preparing for these adjudicated events for both her school orchestra ensembles and her private lesson students. In these letters, she wrote about how she would scaffold repertoire selection by the technical demands of the notation as well as how music competitions were structured and organized in Iowa.[58] Specifically, she would write to her father, commenting on how she was selecting repertoire as a way of mirroring the sequence of instruction she had received. In a letter that she wrote to her parents on March 17, 1929, she stated that "E. Waterloo won 7 first places at Oelwein [Iowa] and 6 second places." Within this letter, she wrote details about how she coached one student in particular, Francis, to compete against other peer performers.

> When Alice [piano accompanist] finishes the introduction, <u>wait</u>. Wait until you feel perfectly at ease before you play your first chord. Hold yourself back ... he said all right. You know, Francis has the brains all right. He did every single thing I told him to the second time he played. Then, when you get over here to this low part, put every ounce of stuff you've got into it. And when you get to the end, <u>don't hold back at all</u>. Turn loose <u>completely</u>.[59]

Music adjudicated events and competitions were valued learning experiences around Waterloo, Iowa. Waterloo East High School Orchestra earned several superior (first division) and excellent (second division) ratings while Elizabeth was the assistant conductor of the orchestras.[60] According to an article appearing in the *Des Moines Register* on May 8, 1931, the reported acknowledge that "East High School's initial first place victory in the state music contest in several years came Thursday [May 7, 1931] when the wind and stringed instrument group was awarded top honors in Iowa City."[61] Similar accolades appear throughout the 1930s in print in various Iowan newspaper outlets, touting the "excellent school training" students received within the orchestra and band music ensembles.

In addition to the Waterloo East High School Orchestra performing at the state level in Iowa, this ensemble also performed at national competitions. The National School Orchestra Association held contests in the 1930s and in 1935, and Elizabeth led her orchestra in a performance at the NSOA competition held in Madison, Wisconsin. The ensemble's previous success was a prediction of their success at this event. The adjudicators, including Howard Hanson and Francis Findlay, had positive feedback about the ensemble performance, stating "the overture was played with great spirit and with a considerable understanding

Figure 1.14 East Waterloo High School Symphony Orchestra, East Waterloo
High School Yearbook, 1939, page 39.
Source: Used with permission by Waterloo Public Schools.

of its musical content ... there seems to be a genuine thrill in the music
which bespeaks a high degree of sincerity."[62]

Not only could Elizabeth lead her students to perform well at the
music competitions, but other music teachers saw her as a master string
pedagogue and invited her, on multiple occasions, to adjudicate other
music teachers' student performances. It is clear that music adjudicated
events and competitions were important learning experiences for
Elizabeth to share with her students.

Professional Performance in Waterloo

Alongside teaching, Elizabeth's practice as a string performer was
an essential component of her life and career. While she was residing
and teaching in Waterloo, Elizabeth was also an active performer in
and around the neighboring communities.[63] During her first few years
of living in Waterloo, Elizabeth often performed with other local
musicians, including Mildred Townsend (instructor of cello and double
bass, Waterloo Public Schools) and Alice Smoker (pianist within their
trio).[64] In her correspondence to her parents, Elizabeth acknowledged
her experiences of being called to perform at the local radio station,
WJAM Radio Waterloo.[65] Elizabeth wrote to her parents that she
had a dedicated time (e.g., in 1928, Thursdays 9:00–9:30 p.m.) for live
broadcasting over the airwaves where she performed with her trio and
as a soloist. There were multiple instances where Elizabeth reported
being called upon to rush down to the radio station recording studio to
provide music during a break between events, and she mentioned that

she was excited for the extra performing opportunities. She remarked in her correspondence to her parents that not all performances were her best and provided a fair evaluation of her flaws; however, this evaluation was never self-deprecating.

In the area around Waterloo, there was a need for a performing ensemble that utilized the talents of the many musicians. From discussions among the musicians, the Waterloo Civic Symphony Orchestra was founded in September 1929; Elizabeth was elected as concertmaster and treasurer.[66] Later that season, and upon settling on the 90 personnel for the orchestra, Elizabeth was moved to the principal viola position to allow for George Kristufek to serve as concertmaster.[67] During the orchestra's second season (1930–1931), Elizabeth served as business manager alongside her new position on the ensemble's Board of Directors. During the first decade of the orchestra's operation, Elizabeth performed as a soloist in 1931 (viola) and 1936 (violin) under the baton of George Dasch of Chicago, the orchestra's new conductor.[68]

In addition to performing as a violist with a chamber ensemble and as concertmaster for the Waterloo Civic Symphony Orchestra, she learned the French horn and clarinet as a means for her own professional development and performed the French horn with the Waterloo

Figure 1.15 Waterloo Symphony, *Waterloo Daily Courier*, Sunday December 5, 1937, Section 12, page 13.

Summer Band.[69] Elizabeth remained an active member of the Waterloo Civic Symphony Orchestra throughout her time in Waterloo.

Graduate Study

Elizabeth applied for graduate study during the 1929–1930 academic year; she was specifically looking for summer-only degree programs within the vicinity of Chicago-Waterloo.[70] By targeting these types of programs, she could remain in her teaching position and not spend too much money on travel.[71] After considering three institutions – the University of Michigan, Northwestern University, and Syracuse University – Elizabeth decided to attend Northwestern University because it was closer to Waterloo and their summer semester was the shortest.[72]

In the summer of 1932, Elizabeth began a master's degree in violin performance. Her first two summers (1932 and 1933) of study included psychology of music, physics of music, music composition, a course named "Feeling the Rhythm," private violin lessons with Arcule Sheasby, and orchestration.[73] Complementing her academic coursework and private lessons, Elizabeth was able to perform with the summer band and orchestra at Northwestern University. In a postcard dated June 21, 1932, she wrote to her parents, explaining that the conductor (Mr. Dasch) had placed her "in the concertmaster's chair!"[74] Despite her nerves and additional chair seating or "placement" exams, Elizabeth was able to keep this important role in the orchestra. Throughout her summers-only degree program, Elizabeth immersed herself in the musician community and soon became a desired performer. She was routinely invited to perform with orchestras around the City of Chicago and most frequently performed with the Columbia Orchestra (Conservatory of Music), led by Mr. Dasch, and was also hired to perform in chamber string ensembles.[75] In a letter to her parents dated June 23, 1938, Elizabeth remarked about her confidence leading an orchestra.

> I am having a good time in Orchestra this year. Somehow my orchestra playing has "arrived" recently. It is so much easier than it used to be – sightreading – and I am beginning to get the "feel" of leading as concertmaster without trying to lead the conductor, too! – That was always my trouble – not being able to lead and follow at the same time.[76]

During her summers at Northwestern, Elizabeth started more intensive study of the viola and double bass. With proximity to the greater

Figure 1.16 Elizabeth Green, pictured center, head turned left, with
          Northwestern University students, circa 1933.
Source: Elizabeth Green Papers (SC-32), Buswell Library Special Collections,
Wheaton, Illinois.

Chicago metropolitan area during her summer graduate study, Elizabeth
regularly communicated with Mr. Clarence Evans (principal violist of
the Chicago Symphony Orchestra) and was invited to perform string
chamber music with small groups of four or five musicians from around
the city. Mr. Evans offered to teach Elizabeth advanced techniques on
the viola and did not charge her a fee until her salary began the following
fall.[77] Serendipitously, Mr. Glenn Cliffe Bainum (Director of Bands,
Northwestern University) overheard Elizabeth practicing double bass
one afternoon in July 1932 and remarked that he needed another double
bass performer with the summer band. Elizabeth described this interaction in a letter addressed to her parents.

> Yesterday when I came out of my afternoon class, on the way home,
> the most gorgeous black roadster pulled up to the curb … he said
> "You aren't Elizabeth Green, are you?" I said "Yes." He said "You

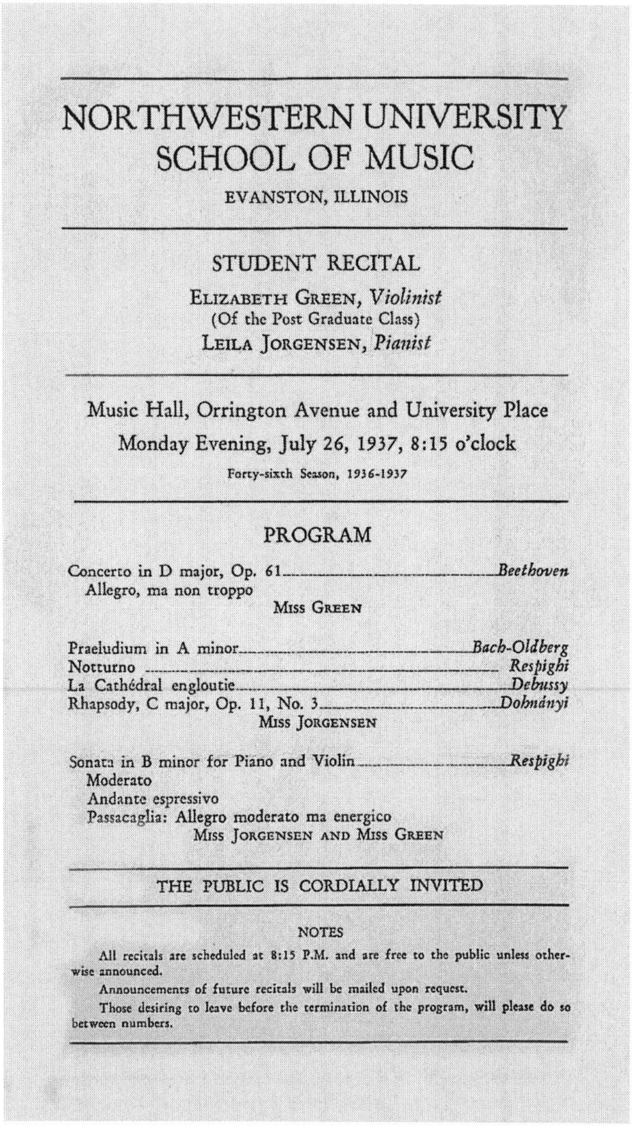

NORTHWESTERN UNIVERSITY
SCHOOL OF MUSIC
EVANSTON, ILLINOIS

STUDENT RECITAL

ELIZABETH GREEN, *Violinist*
(Of the Post Graduate Class)
LEILA JORGENSEN, *Pianist*

Music Hall, Orrington Avenue and University Place

Monday Evening, July 26, 1937, 8:15 o'clock

Forty-sixth Season, 1936-1937

PROGRAM

Concerto in D major, Op. 61..*Beethoven*
Allegro, ma non troppo
MISS GREEN

Praeludium in A minor...*Bach-Oldberg*
Notturno ....*Respighi*
La Cathédral engloutie...*Debussy*
Rhapsody, C major, Op. 11, No. 3..........................*Dohnányi*
MISS JORGENSEN

Sonata in B minor for Piano and Violin.....................*Respighi*
Moderato
Andante espressivo
Passacaglia: Allegro moderato ma energico
MISS JORGENSEN AND MISS GREEN

THE PUBLIC IS CORDIALLY INVITED

NOTES

All recitals are scheduled at 8:15 P.M. and are free to the public unless otherwise announced.

Announcements of future recitals will be mailed upon request.

Those desiring to leave before the termination of the program, will please do so between numbers.

Figure 1.17 Recital Program from July 26, 1937, Elizabeth Green performs Graduate Violin Recital at Northwestern University School of Music and Dramatic Art, age 30.

Source: Elizabeth Green Papers (SC-32), Buswell Library Special Collections, Wheaton, Illinois.

play violin in the orchestra, then?" I said, "Yes, I've been playing Concertmaster this summer." He said, "I wanted to ask you if you'd play bass for our next concert." … so, my reputation as a bass player is stepping up a notch.[78]

Elizabeth's career as a professional musician in the Chicago metropolitan area was enhanced through Mr. Evans' and Mr. Bainum's professional connections and recommendations.

Due to the Great Depression, which impacted Iowa in 1933, Elizabeth had to wait until 1937 to continue her degree program.[79] During this time in history, the Waterloo Bank "failed,"[80] and consequently, she financially supported her parents for the next five years through her concertizing, working as a course grader for Northwestern, writing music reviews for newspapers, and securing personal loans.[81] During her third summer semester, she presented a full graduate recital in lieu of a thesis,[82] and her degree was awarded in January 1939.

Green's Last Year in Waterloo

During the last year in Waterloo, Elizabeth encountered many instances of being called away to other places around the country. It is clear from the correspondence to her parents that Elizabeth was a voracious learner and agreed to many opportunities, including conducting the 1941 Iowa All-State Orchestra. Within her letter dated March 16, 1941, while conducting the Iowa All-State Orchestra, Elizabeth explained to her parents that

> Dr. Lauer, Psychology Department at Ames College, has daughter in the first violin section. Last night he corralled me to see if I'd be interested in coming to the high school there to teach … we had quite the talk![83]

During her guest conducting experience with the Iowa All-State Orchestra, others also took notice of Elizabeth's skill as a teacher and musician. In a letter from David Mattern, Professor of Music Education at the University of Michigan, dated March 26, 1941, Mattern wrote:

> I told my [university] students here that I couldn't remember having attended a finer rehearsal at any time. Your professional command of your instrument and the really inspiring, original suggestions, which you were constantly giving these young players impressed me greatly. … There are few people who can handle strings the way you can do

Figure 1.18 Elizabeth Green leading a string ensemble at the National Music
          Camp, circa 1941.
Source: Elizabeth Green Papers, Bentley Historical Library, University of
Michigan.

it. Incidentally, it is a pleasure to see a lady who can really conduct in
a professional manner and you certainly demonstrated that ability.[84]

In another letter from Joseph Maddy, President of the National Music
Camp, dated April 4, 1941, Maddy wrote:

> I want to tell you how much I enjoyed working with the Iowa All-
> State Orchestra at Des Moines and how greatly I appreciate your
> work. … I hope you will be able to include the National Music
> Camp in your vacation plans this summer. I know that we would
> enjoy seeing you at Interlochen.[85]

Elizabeth performed with many chamber ensembles during her years
employed by East Waterloo Public Schools. Instances included her
performances at the Gordon String Quartet School in Connecticut,[86]
and she recounted her memory of driving through Ann Arbor,
Michigan, while returning home in August 1941:

We came right down Washtenaw Avenue. At that time, the trees were *so* magnificent! Elm trees that were about three stories tall arched right across the street, so that it was just an arch of beautiful trees for a mile down the street. I said that it was a pretty town, and that I might like to teach there some day. And Larry [Fisher] said, "Well, why don't you, Miss Green?"[87]

Approximately nine months later, Elizabeth was hospitalized for several weeks for an undisclosed illness that included a surgical operation.[88] Immediately preceding her illness, she had read a posting for a teaching position at the University of Michigan to begin in the fall 1942. When she was well enough, Elizabeth applied for the position and began corresponding with David Mattern, Professor of Music Education at the University of Michigan. In Professor Mattern's letter to Elizabeth dated February 1, 1942, he wrote: "Nothing would please me more than to find a way to bring you to Ann Arbor."[89] Throughout the next few months, David wrote to Elizabeth about the financial turmoil the university was experiencing and notified her on March 3, 1942, that "it does not look as if there will be expansion in the immediate future. ... The Ann Arbor Public Schools are looking for a full time string teacher with outstanding ability – can you recommend such a person?"[90] Elizabeth expressed significant interest in the Ann Arbor Public School string teaching position and interviewed with Mattern through the Clark-Brewer Teachers Agency; this agency also negotiated her salary and terms of agreement.[91] On May 22, 1942, Otto Haisley, Superintendent of Ann Arbor Public Schools, acknowledged the receipt of Elizabeth's telegram stating that she accepted the teaching position.[92] Elizabeth relocated to Michigan in August 1942 to the next stage of her teaching career in Ann Arbor.

Elizabeth Green influenced the cultural life of Waterloo, Iowa, through her commitment to student musical learning and dedication to live performing arts within this community. Appearing on page seven of the June 9, 1942, issue of the *Waterloo Daily Courier* was an announcement of Elizabeth's resignation from East Waterloo Public Schools, and a few days later, a dedication to her 14-year tenure in Waterloo, Iowa, was printed: "Miss Green has been an able and inspirational teacher ... and in general she has been a tower of strength in the city's musical life."[93] A few days later, a similar laudatory piece was printed in the Editor's Column, stating that "we are very sorry to lose her, but our utmost good will go with her and we confidently predict for her a corresponding success in her new field."[94]

Elizabeth had a close connection to her parents, and this continued when she moved to Ann Arbor. During the next stage of Elizabeth's career, which is detailed in the following chapter, her parents had experienced several setbacks related to their health. Throughout their correspondence to each other during the 1950s, Elizabeth would remind her parents to take good care of themselves and "take their medicine," while also alluding to multiple short-term illnesses. In October 1962, Albert Green passed away at the age of 92. Shortly thereafter (February 1963), Elizabeth's mother passed away at the age of 94.

Notes

1   This statement was included in an editor's note for Elizabeth Green's journal article, "Three Works I Would Hate to Teach Without," *Repertoire* 1, no. 1 (1951): 45.
2   Deborah Annette Smith, "Elizabeth A. H. Green: A Biography," Ph.D. diss., University of Michigan, Ann Arbor, 1986, ProQuest Dissertations & Theses Global (UMI No. 8621380): 1, 7.
3   Smith, 12.
4   Ibid., 9.
5   Elizabeth Green, interview by Deborah A. Smith, February 12, 1985.
6   Ibid.
7   Ibid.
8   Ibid.
9   Smith, 17.
10 Rosagitta Podrovsky, "A History of Music Education in Chicago Public Schools," Ph.D. diss., Northwestern University, Evanston, 1978, ProQuest Dissertations & Theses Global (UMI No. 7907925): 114.
11 Folder 1, Programs, 1914–1928, Box 3, Folder 1. Elizabeth Green Papers, SC-032. Buswell Library Special Collections, Wheaton, Illinois. Accessed May 19, 2021.
12 Elizabeth Green, interview by Deborah A. Smith, February 12, 1985, quoted in Deborah A. Smith, "Elizabeth A. H. Green: A Biography," Ph.D. diss., University of Michigan, Ann Arbor, 1986, ProQuest Dissertations & Theses Global (UMI No. 8621380).
13 Emma Timmerman was not related to Mary Timmerman Green.
14 Elizabeth Green, interview by Deborah A. Smith, February 12, 1985.
15 Folder 16, Biographical, Box 4, Folder 16. Elizabeth Green Papers, SC-032. Buswell Library Special Collections. Accessed May 19, 2021.
16 Smith, 22.
17 *The Tower, 1920*, 35; Reuben H. Donnelly, Co.
18 Smith, 26.
19 *Wheaton College Bulletin*, 38 (2), April 1919, 47.

20 Smith, 26.
21 *The Tower, 1922*, 32.
22 Ibid.
23 Folder 9, Albert Green, 1921–22, Box 11, Folder 9. Elizabeth Green Papers, SC-032. Buswell Library Special Collections. https://archives.wheaton.edu/repositories/2/archival_objects/163399. Accessed July 2, 2019.
24 Smith, 23–24.
25 Smith, 23.
26 Elizabeth Green, interview by Deborah A. Smith, March 18, 1985, quoted in Deborah A. Smith, "Elizabeth A. H. Green: A Biography," Ph.D. diss., University of Michigan, Ann Arbor, 1986, ProQuest Dissertations and Theses Global (UMI No. 8621380).
27 *The Tower, 1927*, 151; Reuben H. Donnelly, Co.; Smith, 27.
28 Telephone conversation with Keith Call, Archivist, Wheaton College, May 19, 2021.
29 "Review," *The Wheaton Progressive*, May 25, 1923.
30 "New Artists Appear in Recital," *Wheaton College Record*, October 1, 1924.
31 Smith, 25.
32 Elizabeth Green, interview by Deborah A. Smith, March 18, 1985.
33 Elizabeth Green interview by Deborah A. Smith, February 12, 1985; Folder 39, Music Education, Schools, Bulletins, Box 1, Folder 39. Elizabeth Green Papers, SC-032. Buswell Library Special Collections. https://archives.wheaton.edu/repositories/2/archival_objects/163390. Accessed July 2, 2019.
34 Smith, 28.
35 "G. T. Bennett Will Leave East High, Plans to Enter College Music Field," *Waterloo Courier*, April 24, 1933, 6.
36 Green interview, February 12, 1985.
37 Smith, 31.
38 Folders 1–5, Correspondence 1928–1929, Bulletins, Box 2, Folders 1–5. Elizabeth Green Papers, SC-032. Buswell Library Special Collections.
39 Ibid.
40 Folder 2, Correspondence 1929, Bulletins, Box 2, Folder 2. Elizabeth Green Papers, SC-032. Buswell Library Special Collections.
41 Ibid.
42 Ibid.
43 Smith, 32.
44 Ibid.
45 The second stage of teaching is often defined by such criteria as number of years of teaching (e.g., 4–10 years of teaching experience). C. I. Kirkpatrick, "To Invest, Coast or Idle: Second-Stage Teachers Enact Their Job Engagement," paper presented at the annual conference of the American Education Research Association, Chicago, IL, April 2007.
46 "G. T. Bennett Will Leave East High, Plans to Enter College Music Field," *Waterloo Courier*, April 24, 1933, 6.
47 Smith, 42.

48 Jacques Gordon (1897–1948), a Russian-born violinist, was known as child prodigy in the early 1900s. He was appointed Concertmaster of the Chicago Symphony Orchestra (1921–1930) and also served as the head of the violin department of the American Conservatory of Music. The first Gordon String Quartet was established in Chicago in 1921 and was high demand as a performing group. In 1930, Gordon founded the Gordon Musical Association and maintained a prestigious summer school of music called Music Mountain (Falls Village, Connecticut).

49 Elizabeth studied with Jacques Gordon, Concertmaster of the Chicago Symphony Orchestra (1921–1930), at his summer school. The summer school was a ten-week experience that included individual instruction on violin and additional music classes.

50 Folder 8, Correspondence 1931, Bulletins, Box 2, Folder 8. Elizabeth Green Papers, SC-032. Buswell Library Special Collections.

51 Ibid. Clarence Evans served as principal violist of the Chicago Symphony Orchestra.

52 Ibid.

53 Folder 9, Correspondence 1932, Bulletins, Box 2, Folder 9. Elizabeth Green Papers, SC-032. Buswell Library Special Collections.

54 Smith, 49–50.

55 "Music Magazine to Have Series by Elizabeth Green," *Waterloo Daily Courier*, September 16, 1936, 5.

56 Grace V. Wilson, "Making the Most of Contests," *Music Supervisors' Journal* 13, no. 2 (1926): 11–65.

57 "G. T. Bennett Will Leave East High, Plans to Enter College Music Field," *Waterloo Courier*, April 24, 1933, 6; Craig Manteuffel, "KSHSAA Board Policy." www.kshsaa.org/public/music/main.cfm. Accessed June 25, 2020.

58 Folders 1–5, Correspondence 1928–1929, Bulletins, Box 2, Folders 1–5. Elizabeth Green Papers, SC-032. Buswell Library Special Collections.

59 Ibid.

60 Ibid.

61 Folder 8, Correspondence 1931, Bulletins, Box 2, Folder 8. Elizabeth Green Papers, SC-032. Buswell Library Special Collections.

62 Folder 29, General 1935, Bulletins, Box 4, Folder 29. Elizabeth Green Papers, SC-032. Buswell Library Special Collections.

63 Ibid., 54.

64 Folders 1–5, Correspondence 1928–1929, Bulletins, Box 2, Folders 1–5. Elizabeth Green Papers, SC-032. Buswell Library Special Collections.

65 Ibid.

66 Smith, 55.

67 Ibid.; Folder 1, Scrapbook for the Waterloo Symphony Orchestra, Bulletins, Box 7, Folder 1. Elizabeth Green Papers, SC-032. Buswell Library Special Collections.

68 Ibid.; "Elizabeth Green Violin Soloist With Symphony," *Waterloo Daily Courier*, March 3, 1936, 7.

69 Ibid.

70 Ibid., 61.
71 Elizabeth Green, interview by Deborah A. Smith, April 2, 1985.
72 Ibid.
73 Smith, 65; Folder 9, Correspondence 1932, Bulletins, Box 2, Folder 9. Elizabeth Green Papers, SC-032. Buswell Library Special Collections.
74 Folder 9, Correspondence 1932, Bulletins, Box 2, Folder 9. Elizabeth Green Papers, SC-032. Buswell Library Special Collections.
75 Ibid.
76 Folder 13, Correspondence 1938, Bulletins, Box 2, Folder 13. Elizabeth Green Papers, SC-032. Buswell Library Special Collections.
77 Folder 9, Correspondence 1932, Bulletins, Box 2, Folder 9. Elizabeth Green Papers, SC-032. Buswell Library Special Collections.
78 Ibid.
79 Folder 12, Correspondence 1937, Bulletins, Box 2, Folder 12. Elizabeth Green Papers, SC-032. Buswell Library Special Collections.
80 Folder 9, Correspondence 1932, Bulletins, Box 2, Folder 9. Elizabeth Green Papers, SC-032. Buswell Library Special Collections.
81 Folder 12, Correspondence 1937, Bulletins, Box 2, Folder 12. Elizabeth Green Papers, SC-032. Buswell Library Special Collections; Folder 9, Correspondence 1932, Bulletins, Box 2, Folder 9. Elizabeth Green Papers, SC-032. Buswell Library Special Collections.
82 Smith, 67.
83 Folder 15, Correspondence 1941, Bulletins, Box 2, Folder 15. Elizabeth Green Papers, SC-032. Buswell Library Special Collections.
84 Folder 12, Correspondence 1939–1952, Bulletins, Box 6, Folder 12. Elizabeth Green Papers, SC-032. Buswell Library Special Collections.
85 Ibid.
86 Folder 15, Correspondence 1941, Bulletins, Box 2, Folder 15. Elizabeth Green Papers, SC-032. Buswell Library Special Collections.
87 Elizabeth Green, interview by Deborah A. Smith, March 11, 1985.
88 Folder 16, Correspondence 1942, Bulletins, Box 2, Folder 16. Elizabeth Green Papers, SC-032. Buswell Library Special Collections.
89 Folder 1, Correspondence 1942, Bulletins, Box 5, Folder 1. Elizabeth Green Papers, SC-032. Buswell Library Special Collections.
90 Ibid.
91 Ibid.
92 Ibid.
93 "Elizabeth Green Accepts Post in Ann Arbor, Mich.," *Waterloo Daily Courier*, June 9, 1942, 7.
94 "Good Wishes, Miss Green," *Waterloo Daily Courier*, June 10, 1942.

2 Elizabeth A. H. Green (1942–1995)

To define it: The job of Music Education is to turn over the soil and find where it is fertile.

To sow the seed, tend it joyously for many patient years, and eventually rejoice in the harvest.[1]

– Elizabeth A. H. Green

The first chapter of this book presented a biographical representation of Elizabeth A. H. Green's life from her birth in 1906 until her relocation from Waterloo, Iowa, to Ann Arbor, Michigan. Based on her life so far, it is clear that Elizabeth led an extraordinary life as a musician and teacher during approximately the first 40 years of the twentieth century. Continuing onward in this chapter, I continue to present biographical information of Elizabeth's career and life in music education. In the first section of the chapter, I present her teaching career in both secondary and tertiary education in Ann Arbor, Michigan. The second section of the chapter includes details of her professional activity during retirement. (I ask the reader to recall the details of this chapter as they proceed to the subsequent chapters of this book.)

The Ann Arbor, Michigan, Years (1942–1974)

Transitioning from Waterloo, Iowa, to Ann Arbor, Michigan

Arriving approximately one week before classes began for the fall 1942 semester, Elizabeth and her mother, Mary Green, drove from Waterloo, Iowa, to Ann Arbor, Michigan; As remarked in a previous interview, she was "just thrilled" to be joining the faculty of the Ann Arbor Public Schools (AAPS) and the University of Michigan.[2] In a letter dated

DOI: 10.4324/9781003152415-2

April 17, 1987, Elizabeth remarked about the financial hardship she encountered during the summer of 1942, stating:

> This year, September to June, 1942, was the most difficult financially of my entire teaching career. I took a "$2000.00" salary cut to come to Ann Arbor, I had promised my parents that if I took the job, I would send home $100.00 a month. I had expected Ann Arbor Salary to run on a ten month basis. When I got there, I found they paid on the twelve month basis – much less each month than I had expected.

Despite the financial hardship, Elizabeth was able to locate an apartment "so that we could be together again [928 Oakland Avenue]."[3] From this statement, and as she was raised in a tradition that cared for family members, it is clear that Elizabeth intended for her parents to join her in Ann Arbor.

After locating housing in Ann Arbor, Elizabeth learned of a former colleague from Waterloo, Laura Hamann, that was teaching physical education in the AAPS. The two former colleagues reminisced about the history of Waterloo while sharing dinner, and Elizabeth learned of the small enrollment in the Ann Arbor High School Orchestra.[4] Elizabeth knew that there was much music ensemble building to do.[5]

Teaching at Ann Arbor High School, Elementary, and Junior High Schools (1942–1953)

Elizabeth was excited to begin teaching and building the orchestras in Ann Arbor, and during her first year of teaching, she started 100 students on string instruments.[6] Her assignment was teaching orchestra at Ann Arbor High School (AAHS), among other school buildings, and her first goal was to increase the membership from the 13 members when she arrived. As of May 31, 1942, band instruments were not being manufactured because metal was a war-rationed product; however, wood was not,[7] and after Elizabeth's first year of teaching in Ann Arbor, the orchestra doubled its personnel. According to the AAHS 1943 Yearbook, "great progress was shown this year, largely because of the enthusiastic conducting of Miss Elizabeth Green, new to Ann Arbor from Waterloo, Iowa."[8] During her first five years at AAHS, the enrollment of the orchestra increased because of three factors: (1) Elizabeth's recruitment efforts; (2) the end of World War II; and (3) a new rehearsal schedule that moved the ensemble from afterschool, once a week, into the school day, every day.[9]

Figure 2.1 Elizabeth Green (violin) with Mr. Charles Yates (clarinet) and Miss
Rose Marie Grentzer (piano).
Source: Used with permission by MLive Media Group, 1944.

Elizabeth's recruitment efforts and teaching continued to increase
enrollment of the AAHS Orchestra. According the AAHS 1945
Yearbook,

> the orchestra, growing steadily under the capable baton of Miss
> Elizabeth Green, turned in a number of fine performances during
> the year ... without doubt the highlight of the year was the out-
> standing performance of this group in the operetta.[10]

Creating a comprehensive string education program and increasing
enrollment was a challenging task, and to accomplish this task, Elizabeth
knew that she needed to increase the visibility of the string ensembles

within the community.[11] Broadly, Elizabeth's strategy for increasing visibility was to present programs with her high school orchestra students at the local elementary and junior high schools. This strategy yielded 100 beginning string students during her first year.[12] Elizabeth's desire to increase the visibility of string education throughout the State of Michigan incorporated this local strategy of presenting programs while engaging string quartets from the University of Michigan School of Music.[13] Additionally, Elizabeth planned to highlight string music education at the statewide band and orchestra clinic with a colleague, Clyde Vroman, Instructor of Music Education at the University of Michigan and the orchestra instructor at the University High School.[14] She remarked:

> We decided to get all the kids in the city together that could play strings at all. So, we had the ballroom at the Union and we put out a hundred-piece orchestra. We started [the concert] with everyone playing. The high school kids were seated in front and other kids were farmed out in the acres around. We started playing tunes like the "Little Waltz" from *Tune-A-Day*. Everybody played and they played in tune. It made a big sound. ... Then we played a little harder tune, and we ended up with just the high school students playing one or two rather decent pieces. Dr. Vroman and I took turns conducting that performance.[15]

Elizabeth was often looking for ways to make string music education more visible to the public, and the 1940s were an important time in history for the advancement of string music education.

Elizabeth believed that in order for interest in stringed instrument performance, the orchestra needed to be visible within the community, and firstly, she thought performance opportunities were great publicity for string music education. As a way of expanding the performance opportunities for the orchestra students of AAPS, Elizabeth coordinated large festival programs combining students enrolled in music classes from all of the AAPS into their Annual May Festival program, presented at Hill Auditorium on the campus of the University of Michigan.

Additionally, Elizabeth organized demonstration concerts for the Parent–Teacher Association (PTA) of Ann Arbor to showcase the students of Slauson Junior High School and a few beginning string classes.[16] As another way of expanding visibility, Elizabeth also allowed preservice music teachers attending the University of Michigan to observe her orchestra classes. In a letter written to her parents, dated October 6, 1942, Elizabeth wrote:

Figure 2.2 Elizabeth Green conducting the 1944 AAPS All-City Orchestra.
Source: Used with permission by MLive Media Group.

Figure 2.3 Elizabeth Green conducting the 1949 AAPS All-City Orchestra.
Source: Used with permission by Ann Arbor Public Library.

Dr. Mattern brough one of his classes out to Mack School this morning to hear my very first class session with a group of my beginners. ... He said to me, "I am so happy to have my classes get to hear an expert like you."[17]

By 1951, the AAHS Orchestra had 61 students enrolled.[18] A third way of expanding the orchestra's visibility was through music competitions or festivals. Given Elizabeth's strongly held core beliefs about music performance, the orchestra began and continued to earn top ratings at the large group music festivals. Alongside her work with the high school, Elizabeth was also promoting string education programs in Ann Arbor's elementary and junior high schools.[19] Her teaching assignment included Slauson Junior High School, and her recruitment efforts also increased the enrollment of the orchestra from 9 to 45 in 1953.[20] During the 1953–1954 school year, Elizabeth transitioned away from full-time teaching with the AAPS (a 0.4 FTE position) to full-time teaching with the University of Michigan.[21]

According to Elizabeth, one essential component of a comprehensive string education program is private instrument study. She offered lessons to any student who wanted to study violin privately.[22] To Elizabeth, private instrument study allowed for accelerated technical advancement on the instrument when partnered with school-based string orchestra classes. Throughout the early years of working in Ann Arbor, Elizabeth

Figure 2.4 Slauson Junior High Orchestra, circa 1948.

Source: Elizabeth Green Papers, Bentley Historical Library, University of Michigan.

had a private lesson studio ranging from 15 to 25 students, including notable performers such as Michael and Charles Avsharian.[23]

Teaching at the University of Michigan

Joint teaching positions between the AAPS District and the University of Michigan were commonplace during this time in history. Dr. Clyde Vroman is one example; Miss Marguerite Hood is another. As Elizabeth explained in a letter:

> The war had started in December of 1941. In September of 1942, I started to teach for Ann Arbor Public Schools and the University of Michigan ... to set up an adequate strings and orchestra department in the Ann Arbor Public Schools. For this reason I was on a split salary, schools and university, for some years. As I got things built up in the schools, my time allotment gradually changed in favor of more University teaching until finally I was no longer in the schools.[24]

Both Elizabeth Green and Marguerite Hood joined the faculty of the University of Michigan in fall 1942; however, Marguerite joined as Assistant Professor of Music Education (half-time) and served as Supervisor of Music for AAPS (a joint position she would maintain from 1942 to 1958).[25] Elizabeth Green's tenure with the University of Michigan spanned more than three decades. Below, I document Elizabeth's journey as a university professor until her retirement in 1975.

Instructor in Music Education (1942–1948)

Elizabeth Green was first hired by the University of Michigan in October 1942 as a one-tenth-time Instructor of Music. According to the University Bulletin, her salary for both fall and spring terms was $200.00.[26] Even though she was hired, she did not teach in the School of Music until 1944.[27] Elizabeth continued teaching for the School of Music in the next few years, and the administration would gradually release more teaching and responsibilities to her. During the first few years of her employment with the University of Michigan, Elizabeth was hired during the summer session to teach a course named School Orchestra Materials. In 1946, her teaching load increased to one-eighth-time and then one-fourth-time during the spring term. By 1948, Elizabeth was hired as a half-time Assistant Professor of Music Education in the School of Music for a three-year period.[28] According the minutes from

Figure 2.5 Elizabeth Green, circa 1953.
Source: Elizabeth Green Papers, Bentley Historical Library, University of Michigan.

the School of Music Executive Committee Meeting on April 20, 1948, Dr. Earl V. Moore reported the approval of the Provost for the promotion of Miss Elizabeth Green to the position of Assistant Professor.

Assistant Professor of Music (1948–1958)

In the fall of 1948, Elizabeth began her full-time faculty post as Assistant Professor of Music Education. During this time in rank, she became increasingly interested in preservice music teacher development while still maintaining an active career as a professional conductor. Elizabeth became involved with the American String Teachers Association, and her concern for the welfare of present and future string students was evident in her work with this association.[29] In order to dedicate her time to preservice music teacher education, Elizabeth decided to resign from her secondary school teaching responsibilities with AAPS and assume additional teaching responsibilities with the University of Michigan.[30] From 1953 to 1956, Elizabeth taught only string classes at Eberwhite Elementary School, and in 1956, she resigned from AAPS to begin a full-time teaching assignment at the School of Music.[31] She remarked:

> When I gave them up, I was ready to give them up. I'd done enough college teaching to know that there were lots of other people that could do the fine work in the public schools, and that it was time for me to pass what I knew to them ... the next generation of teachers.[32]

Her resignation concluded a twenty-eight-year career of public school teaching.

As Elizabeth reallocated her time away from public school teaching to preservice music teacher education, the School of Music was experiencing an increase in enrollment.[33] As a result, Elizabeth was reassigned to teach conducting courses for instrumental music education majors. At this time, she was already teaching the elementary conducting sequence (course Nos. 137 and 138) and directing the instrumental music student teachers. With the hiring of Allen P. Britton (instrumental music teacher educator, assistant professor, and lecturer in the School of Education) in 1950, Elizabeth's teaching schedule changed in the fall of 1953. She continued to teach elementary conducting classes and added two classes of "Violin 1" and "Violin 2" for non-string majors.[34]

Associate Professor of Music (1958–1963)

In the fall of 1957, the University of Michigan Board of Regents approved Elizabeth's promotion, and beginning in fall 1958, she was promoted from Assistant Professor to Associate Professor.[35] She continued her previous teaching schedule during her time as an associate professor and offered a variety of summer courses, including "Special Problems in Teaching String Instruments" and "Survey of School Orchestra Materials and Processes."[36] In 1959, Elizabeth's teaching schedule was modified to include a methods course titled "Fundamentals of Teaching Instrumental Music." This course had been previously taught by David Mattern,[37] and this course's laboratory component was located at the University Elementary School.[38]

Elizabeth was an innovator, and as an associate professor, she created new courses for the music education majors at the University of Michigan, including "Advanced Conducting for Secondary School Orchestras" (Music Ed. 139).[39] During the summer of 1961, she offered this course and continued to create new courses for the students and

Figure 2.6 Elizabeth Green, circa 1958.
Source: Elizabeth Green Papers, Bentley Historical Library, University of Michigan.

to advance string music education. In the winter semester of 1962, she created a new string methods course (Music Ed. 121) to replace the former two courses titled "Strings 1" and "Strings 2."[40]

Professor of Music (1963–1974)

In the spring of 1963, the University of Michigan Board of Regents approved Elizabeth's promotion, and beginning in fall 1963, she was promoted from Associate Professor to Professor of Music.[41] For the most part, Elizbeth's teaching schedule remained unchanged for the final 11 years as a faculty member of the School of Music.[42] These courses typically included conducting (course Nos. 300, 301, 401, 501), music education courses (course No. D-370, "University Elementary

Figure 2.7 Elizabeth Green playing violin, circa 1965.
Source: Used with permission by MLive Media Group.

School"), violin classes (course Nos. 111, 112, and 121), and private applied string lessons.[43] At this point in Elizabeth's career, the School of Music was experiencing significant growth in music education majors, and she found herself teaching multiple sections of her courses to accommodate the growth.[44]

In 1951, the university began planning the development of property acquired by the University of Michigan, north of the Huron River. These development plans included a new School of Music building. This new facility, named the Earl V. Moore Building, opened its doors in summer 1964, and Elizabeth taught all but one of her courses in this new building.[45] Immediately following her sabbatical leave (1964–1965), Elizabeth was notified that her course assignments might be reassigned to strings and might not include music education or conducting. In a letter addressed to Dean of the School of Music, Jim Wallace, she wrote:

> To make a step into the String Department this autumn … is some-thing I'm willing to do – in fact, have already started – but under no circumstances do I wish to give up my conducting classes. These

are, without exception, my greatest contribution to this University, and the reputation of this phase of my work is rapidly growing into something that I believe will make us not unhappy in the future. My conducting book is gradually becoming the authority in this field and is beginning to attract international recognition. Certainly, I do not want to see this line of progress interrupted now ... [conducting] is the one thing I have in my teaching schedule that is musically challenging to myself.[46]

For the next decade, Elizabeth continued to teach music education courses; during this time, she offered private conducting lessons for graduate students as well as advanced conducting classes.[47]

Elizabeth's final semester teaching at the University of Michigan was the summer of 1974; however, she took the university's retirement furlough, with the final academic year (1974–1975) used to conduct research.[48] Elizabeth has achieved what few have done or will do during their professional lives and has attained national and international distinction in two fields of music – the teaching of stringed instruments and the teaching of conducting.

Professional Performance in Ann Arbor

Elizabeth Green believed that applied music performance and music education were inextricably linked. Alongside her public school teaching career, she was a dedicated string performer and instrumental music conductor. As previously documented in Chapter 1, her career as a performer flourished while living in Waterloo, Iowa. In the following section, I will document a select few performance experiences throughout her career while living in Ann Arbor.

As soon as Elizabeth relocated to Ann Arbor, news of her arrival permeated the musician community living in southeast Michigan. During one of Dr. Joseph Maddy's many visits to her classroom at AAHS, he asked her to play violin with the Ann Arbor Civic Orchestra. In a letter addressed to her parents on September 27, 1942, Elizabeth wrote:

> Dr. Maddy dropped by in to the High School Friday afternoon and I met him in the hall on his way to the department. He came in to my office and we had a nice little chat. He conducts the "city symphony" here, which I understand is not very good ... he would like me to play with them ... and also conduct the string sectionals.[49]

Approximately a year later, Elizabeth was a featured soloist; according to an article from the *Ann Arbor News*, dated June 11, 1943, "Elizabeth Green, concertmaster and assistant director of the Ann Arbor Civic Orchestra (later named the Ann Arbor Symphony Orchestra), was named as the organization's most valuable player at a meeting and rehearsal of the orchestra."[50] This was the first of many instances that Elizabeth was a featured soloist with the Civic Symphony Orchestra. Elizabeth performed with this orchestra from 1942 to 1962.[51]

During her first semester teaching in Ann Arbor, Elizabeth was invited to perform on viola with the University of Michigan Symphony Orchestra, due to the low enrollment of the viola section.[52] Elizabeth's teaching schedule with the public school district was full, alongside her full private applied violin lesson studio; she could only attend Friday rehearsals, which lasted approximately two hours. Faculty performing beside their students was commonplace during this time within institutions of higher learning.

Figure 2.8 Elizabeth Green, holding her 235-year-old Montagnana violin, studies music for a performance with the Ann Arbor Civic Orchestra, of which she is returning from 13 years not performing with the ensemble, as the concertmaster *Ann Arbor News*, November 1, 1965.

Source: Used with permission by MLive Media Group.

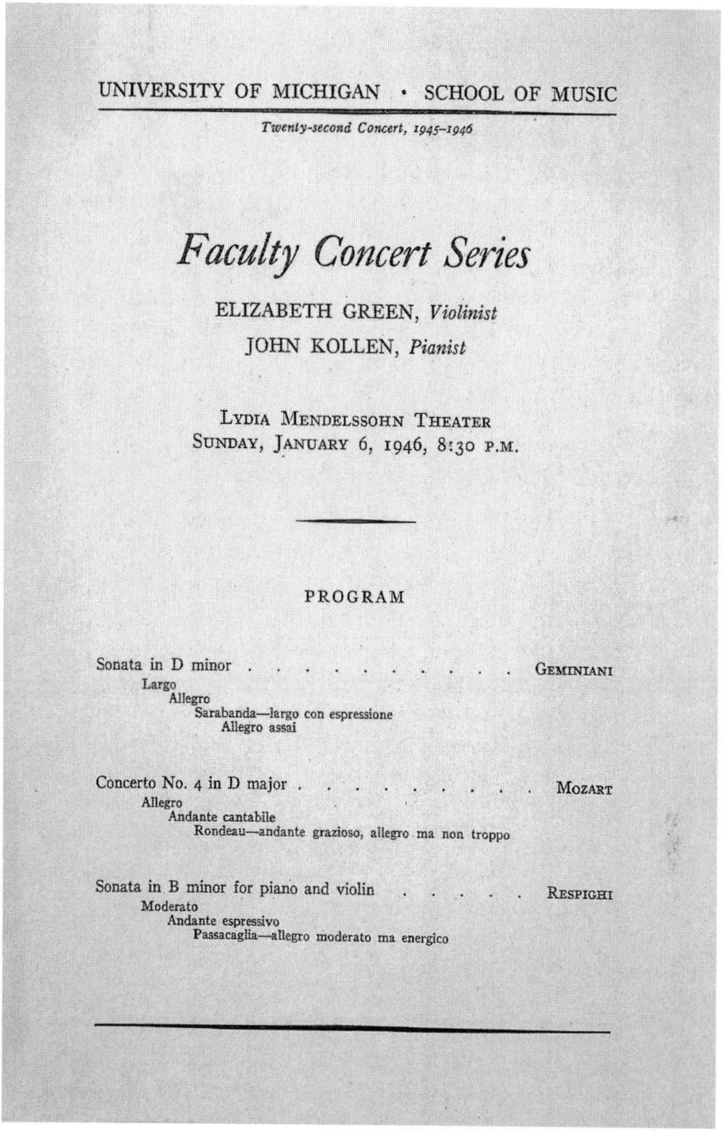

UNIVERSITY OF MICHIGAN · SCHOOL OF MUSIC

Twenty-second Concert, 1945–1946

Faculty Concert Series

ELIZABETH GREEN, *Violinist*

JOHN KOLLEN, *Pianist*

LYDIA MENDELSSOHN THEATER
SUNDAY, JANUARY 6, 1946, 8:30 P.M.

PROGRAM

Sonata in D minor . . . . GEMINIANI
    Largo
        Allegro
            Sarabanda—largo con espressione
            Allegro assai

Concerto No. 4 in D major . . . . MOZART
    Allegro
        Andante cantabile
            Rondeau—andante grazioso, allegro ma non troppo

Sonata in B minor for piano and violin . . . . . RESPIGHI
    Moderato
        Andante espressivo
            Passacaglia—allegro moderato ma energico

Figure 2.9 Recital Program from January 6, 1946, Elizabeth Green performs a
Faculty Recital at University of Michigan School of Music, age 39.

Source: Elizabeth Green Papers (SC-32), Buswell Library Special Collections,
Wheaton, Illinois.

Lastly, and similarly to her time in Waterloo, Elizabeth was a frequent recitalist throughout the United States. One of her first recitals of technically demanding repertoire in Ann Arbor was on January 6, 1946, and she continued to perform regularly during her career in higher education.

Although there were no reviews of her recital in the *Ann Arbor News*, subsequent articles, announcing Green offering a solo recital, mention her artistry. For instance, on July 17, 1953, in the *Kentucky Kernel*, an unknown journalist wrote that "Miss Green is known nationally both for her ability in developing young string players and as a violinist."[53] Another review of her solo recital in Waterloo captured her performance: "Her tone is exquisite and Miss Green played with the kind of vigor and strength one expects of a male musician, despite the liquid character of her playing."[54]

Professional Conducting and Conducting Studies

One very influential mentor to Elizabeth Green was Nicoli Malko. Malko, a native of Russia, studied under Rimsky-Korsakoff, Glazounoff, Liadoff, and Felix Mottl. In Russia he held two major conducting positions, first as the conductor of the Imperial State Opera and Ballet in St. Petersburg, then of the State Philharmonic Orchestra of Leningrad. In recognition of his outstanding conducting skill and reputation as a musician-leader, Malko made his debut in the United States in January 1940, as guest conductor of the Boston Symphony Orchestra, where he was lauded by critics as one of the great conductors of his generation.

While attending the Gordon String Quartet School in summer of 1941, Elizabeth had asked a peer, Thor Johnson, how she could improve her conducting skills. Johnson, who studied conducting with Serge Koussevitsky at Tanglewood, had formerly studied with Malko and recommend that Elizabeth contact him.[55]

> So, on my back from our studies with Mr. Gordon, Mr. Malko was conducting a concert with the Women's Symphony and Mrs. [Clarence] Evans played in the symphony. So, I ran backstage and got hold of her. She took me and introduced me to Mr. Malko, and I told him that I wanted to study with him and I lived in Iowa. He said "All right. If you will write me a letter, we'll set up a time."[56]

Elizabeth began her studies with Malko in the summer of 1941, attending the Malko Workshop of Conducting and Opera.

𝔘𝔫𝔦𝔳𝔢𝔯𝔰𝔦𝔱𝔶 𝔬𝔣 𝔎𝔢𝔫𝔱𝔲𝔠𝔨𝔶

MUSIC DEPARTMENT

presents

ELIZABETH GREEN, Violinist

PHILIP HOMER BARNES, Accompanist

Assisted by

THE UNIVERSITY STRING QUARTET

Memorial Auditorium

WEDNESDAY, JULY 26, 1950

8:00 P.M.

PROGRAM

I

Concerto No. 3 in G Major for Violin . . . . Mozart
  Allegro
  Adagio
  Rondeau: Allegro
                    MISS GREEN

II

Interlude (in Ancient Mode) . . . . Glazounow
Minuetto (Quartet, Opus 54, No. 1) . . . . Haydn
Presto (Quartet, Opus 18, No. 2) . . . . Beethoven

KENNETH WRIGHT, First Violin   MARVIN RABIN, Viola
MARIAN BRODSKY, Second Violin   GORDON KINNEY, Violoncello

III

Allegro . . . . Fiocco
Meditation . . . . Glazounow
Banjo and Fiddle . . . . Kroll
                    MISS GREEN

Ushers are members of Phi Mu Alpha, Men's Honorary Fraternity

Thursday, July 27, Student Ensemble Music Program
Memorial Hall, 8 p.m.

Friday, July 28, String Orchestra Concert, Summer Clinic
Memorial Hall Amphitheatre, 8 p.m.

Figure 2.10 Recital Program from July 26, 1950, Elizabeth Green performs a Guest Recital at University of Kentucky Music Department, age 43.

Source: Elizabeth Green Papers (SC-32), Buswell Library Special Collections, Wheaton, Illinois.

The Malko Workshop of Conducting and Opera was a seven-week intensive course (with a short course option, 3.5 weeks in length) that started on June 23 and concluded on August 8, 1941. Nicoli Malko taught and organized this workshop alongside his conducting engagement at Ravinia Music Festival (Ravinia, Illinois) and taught collaboratively with Max Rudolf and John Daggett Howell.[57] Although it is unclear which course Elizabeth enrolled in, it is plausible that she enrolled in the conducting course. Topics within this course included eurythmics; technique of time beating; elements of conducting technique; score reading; conductor in the theater; opera conducting; and practice sessions with live musicians.[58]

In addition to this course, Elizabeth started private conducting lessons and repertoire coaching with Malko. In response to Elizabeth's letter, Malko agreed to a two-hour lesson on a Saturday afternoon in September 1941.[59] Elizabeth vividly recalled her first conducting lesson.

> He sat at the piano and had me beat a measure of three or four, and then he started teaching me. When we started out, he saw that I needed control. I was using all these circular motions which nobody had ever told me about, and which many people still use. So, we started doing physical exercises, and the thought ran thought my mind, "Well, either he's crazy or I am. But I'm paying for this, so I am going to do it!" I had never seen anything like it.[60]

In correspondence between Elizabeth and her parents, she mentioned attending performances conducted by Malko the following summer (1942) in Grand Rapids, Michigan.[61] Elizabeth also mentioned that Malko was "extremely patient, very kind, and … a tremendous teacher [who] knew thoroughly what to teach and how to teach it. He insisted upon perfection … nothing would satisfy him other than that."[62]

During the next five years, Elizabeth continued to take private conducting lessons and maintained a friendship with Malko and also took music notation composition lessons with Dr. Sowerby.[63] In June 1947, Elizabeth traveled to Chicago to study with Malko and to work on a translation of his new book entitled *The Conductor and His Baton*. The book was originally written in Russian and later translated to English by Elizabeth, published in 1950. In a letter to her parents, she wrote: "Mr. Malko's book is really something and embodies all of his wonderfully fine school or method of conducting. It is filled with pictured illustrations and conducting diagrams and some musical examples."[64]

Sabbatical Leave (1964–1965)

As Elizabeth advanced her career and earned promotion from Assistant Professor to Associate Professor with tenure at the University of Michigan, she was granted a year-long sabbatical leave during the 1964–1965 academic year. She planned for this year to study advanced conducting techniques by spending the year away from the university in Europe – Paris, France was her temporary home.[65] In a note that Elizabeth drafted in 1987 to the readers of her special paper collection, she mentioned that "Paris was my home during this time. I traveled for a week or two at a time to other cities to hear the rehearsals under famous conductors and to investigate the teaching of conducting."[66] Throughout this year away from the United States, she wrote numerous letters to her Aunt Florence, who became a surrogate parent after Elizabeth's parents died, and Dr. Allen Britton, Associate Dean of the School of Music at the University of Michigan. In these letters, Elizabeth mentioned traveling to Manchester, England (c. December 16, 1964); Vienna, Austria (c. February 19, 1965); Brussels, Belgium; London, England; and finally Copenhagen, Denmark for the first Nicoli Malko International Conductors' Competition May 17–19, 1965, where she lectured on the Malko teaching methods.[67]

In addition to observing rehearsals led by well-known conductors, Elizabeth took advanced orchestra and conducting courses at the National Conservatoire Supérieur de Musique in Paris and also conducted lessons with Nadia Boulanger. In a letter to her Aunt Florence, Elizabeth remarked that

> she [Boulanger] is one of the truly great women of the world ... the class meets only on Wednesday afternoons at her apartment. The class is about 40 minutes long and she speaks partly in French and partly in English – I'm so fortunate to have this opportunity.[68]

Professional Conducting and Teaching Across the World

National Music Camp at the Interlochen Center for the Arts

Elizabeth's strong reputation as a remarkable pedagogue permeated most of the United States throughout the mid-20th century. In addition to her full-time job teaching in the public schools and the University of Michigan, Elizabeth began teaching summer courses at the National Music Camp at the Interlochen Center for the Arts in the summer of 1943. Founded in 1928, the Interlochen Center for the Arts served to encourage growth in school music programs. In her first summer (1943), she was asked to conduct the Clinic String Orchestra.[69] Over the four-week session, she led the orchestra in three performances and returned the next summer (1944) to continue leading the orchestra.[70,71] During her fifth summer (1947) teaching at the National Music Camp, Elizabeth was asked to teach college division courses as well as rehearsals for the All-State Orchestra. In her letters addressed to her parents, she mentioned taking the 15 college students to the new electronics laboratory. The laboratory housed a cathode-ray oscilloscope that would visually project sound waves.[72] Elizabeth was fascinated by this technology and would test her tone production theories to see if her beliefs were true. These experiences in the laboratory prompted her to write an unpublished manuscript entitled *Physics of Music*.[73] The next few summers, Elizabeth served as the University of Michigan All-State Orchestra guest conductor and received many accolades, including one from Associate Dean Allen Britton, stating "your students were enthusiastic, and I know that you have set some standards and done some grand work, once again for

Figure 2.11 Elizabeth Green leading musicians at National Music Camp, circa 1945.

Source: Elizabeth Green Papers, Bentley Historical Library, University of Michigan.

Figure 2.12 Front cover of 1946 National Music Camp at Interlochen, Michigan brochure.

Source: Elizabeth Green Papers (SC-32), Buswell Library Special Collections, Wheaton, Illinois.

the promotion of better orchestras."[74] Elizabeth served the Interlochen Center for the Arts for decades in various roles (e.g., instructor, observer, clinician). Throughout her time visiting Interlochen, she influenced countless musicians through her instruction and mentoring.

Throughout her career and retirement, Elizabeth served as a guest conductor and teacher in multiple engagements each year around the world, and it is probable that she completed over 500 guest engagements over the course of her career. Unfortunately, documenting all of her professional conducting and teaching across the world is not possible; however, there is documentation of some of these experiences captured in the news media, University of Michigan professional activity reports, and written correspondence. What follows is a cross-section of her professional creative activities throughout her career, including guest teaching and/or speaking engagements and guest conducting work.

Guest Teaching/Speaking Engagements

One of the earliest documented teaching or speaking engagements was in 1946, when Elizabeth traveled to Indianola, Iowa, to present a string clinic to the music majors attending Simpson College. At the invitation of Paul Rolland, Elizabeth was thrilled to attend. Another early teaching engagement was in the summer of 1948 at the Arthur Jordan Conservatory, Butler University (Indianapolis, Indiana). In a letter to her parents, Elizabeth wrote: "it was a 3-day teaching contract ... teaching from 1–3 p.m.,"[75] teaching instrumental music education courses and conducting. Teaching engagements would continue throughout Elizabeth's teaching career; one such engagement was at the University of Connecticut in 1978. During her visit to the university campus, she delivered two keynote speeches on the topic of conducting that were recorded; she led a group in conductor movement fundamentals and also presented a lecture on music teaching and learning.[76]

Guest Conducting Engagements

One of the earliest documented conducting engagements was in March 1941 in Des Moines, Iowa. Elizabeth was asked to lead the Iowa All-State Orchestra at the Iowa Music Educators Association' (IMEA) annual conference. Elizabeth wrote to her parents, explaining "there are 250 in the all-state orchestra ... had a lot of fun when I handled the 1st violin sectional yesterday – 39 first fiddles."[77]

After Elizabeth relocated to Ann Arbor, her out-of-state guest conducting engagements increased, perhaps due to her association with the University of Michigan. In 1948, she had two out-of-state guest conducting appearances with the Indiana and Virginia All-State Orchestras held on October 22, 1948, and December 5, 1948, respectively.[78] Little information exists beyond what is stated within these two announcements appearing in the *Ann Arbor News*; however, additional detail exists in Elizabeth's letters to her parents. In a letter dated December 4, 1948, Elizabeth stated

> The orchestra is excellent! – far superior to my hopes, – and we are having fine sessions. There will be six hours of rehearsals today! Instrumentation is
>   36 first violins
>   36 or more seconds
>   16 cellos
>   16 violas
>   <u>14 basses</u>
>   118 players
>   Can hardly get on the stage! Caliber of the players is really excellent.

Figure 2.13 Elizabeth Green leading musicians at North Dakota "Class A" High School Orchestra Festival in Devil's Lake, North Dakota, April 11, 1958.

Source: Elizabeth Green Papers, Bentley Historical Library, University of Michigan.

Figure 2.14 North Dakota "Class A" High School Orchestra Festival concert in Devil's Lake, North Dakota, April 11, 1958.

Source: Elizabeth Green Papers, Bentley Historical Library, University of Michigan.

Elizabeth had many more out-of-state conducting engagements, including the Kentucky All-State High School String Orchestra (July 17, 1953) and the North Dakota "Class A" High School Orchestra Festival held in Devil's Lake, April 11, 1958.

Elizabeth's reputation of excellence in music leadership did not go unnoticed in the state of Michigan. For instance, Elizabeth was asked to bring her school string orchestra to the 1948 Music Educators National Conference (MENC) held in Detroit, Michigan. In a letter to Elizabeth from Luther Richman on May 21, 1948, he thanked Elizabeth "for the splendid string orchestra program you conducted at our Detroit convention. … More power to you and the string committee in their efforts in this area of music learning."[79]

Professional Violin Studies

From a young age, Elizabeth took her violin studies very seriously, and her dedication to the instrument did not wane when she began her public school teaching position in Waterloo. Besides becoming fluent in the other classical string instruments (e.g., viola, cello, and bass), Elizabeth focused the majority of her practice and advancement on violin technique and repertoire study. In this section of the chapter, I will outline Elizabeth's professional studies and personal relationship with European violin performer Ivan Galamian.

Elizabeth dedicated 13 summers to violin with Ivan Galamian at Meadowmount School of Music.[80] The Meadowmount School of Music, housed in a lodge in rural upstate New York, was established by Galamian in 1944. Despite its humble beginnings, hosting Galamian's private violin students, Meadowmount began to gain prominence among violin pedagogues around the world. Child violin performer prodigy Michael Rabin, for instance, attended in the late 1940s when he was 12 years old, and Elizabeth mentions in her letters that he was "a stunning performer."[81]

Elizabeth's first summer attending Meadowmount was in August 1947, for two weeks. During her time attending Meadowmount, she remarked to her parents: "there is no comparison, Mr. Galamian is so far ahead. It simply floors you to hear this from everyone ... but also with music and superb technique."[82] This quote represents one of Galamian's philosophy about music performance and highly influenced Elizabeth's future teaching. During her first summer of study, Elizabeth learned that Malko and Galamian were acquaintances. Galamian mentioned to Elizabeth that "Mr. Malko was head of the conservatoire in Russia when I graduated." Later that month, a former colleague in Iowa, Paul Rolland (University of Illinois, formerly of Simpson College), arrived at Meadowmount. Meadowmount would prove to be a space where the world's leading string pedagogues would assemble to advance their art and reconnect with each other.

In Elizabeth's second summer attending Meadowmount, in a letter written on August 14, 1948, she commented:

> [Mr. Galamian] did not see how music could be divorced from technique! In all the etudes he himself had studied this summer, Mr. Galamian kept stirring the musical side, – the natural crescendos, the emphasis on certain "bars" notes, etc. ... I would say the distinctive feature of Mr. G's teaching is the perfect system he has worked out for getting everything into the playing in a logical order. Each thing he teaches forms the basis for the next big step, technically and musically. There is just no wasted motion.[83]

In one of her final letters to her parents that summer, Green wrote that she attributes Galamian for giving her so many new ideas to consider.

She wrote "I have an understanding and already a skill I've never felt before. Mr. G says 'Teaching violin is no longer guess work. It is now an exact science.'"[84]

Meadowmount continued to be a space where string pedagogues and performers would assemble, and a few years later (August 1950), Elizabeth commented on the international attraction Meadowmount was garnering. She wrote:

> there are 12 countries represented here this summer. I surely do love it here. And even with the intensive practice ... there is a feeling of pressure – that it has to be done immediately which is good for me after the fast pace of the year.[85]

Elizabeth was very drawn to Galamian, his technique, and his pedagogy. Likewise, Galamian took a special interest in Elizabeth. In August 1951, Elizabeth extended her stay at Meadowmount to get to know the Galamians (Ivan and Judith), and their friendship thrived in the upcoming years.

Disseminating Knowledge Through Publication

As a specialist in the teaching of stringed instruments and conducting, Elizabeth Green wrote a large number of textbooks and articles used widely throughout the world. Her work as a teacher of conducting has gained her national and international prominence; hundreds of her former students now serve as conductors in secondary schools and colleges, and many others are conductors of professional instrumental music ensembles. In almost 70 years of teaching, Elizabeth made several contributions to string instrument and conducting pedagogy. In the following section, I first highlight her contributions to stringed instrument pedagogy and then her contributions to conducting pedagogy.

Elizabeth was not only an accomplished string performer, but also a gifted teacher of string instruments. She is credited with assisting with Galamian's books, *Principles of Violin Playing and Teaching* (1962) and *Teaching String Instruments* (1966) and regularly wrote for periodicals, including the *American String Teacher*, *School Musician*, *The Etude*, *The Instrumentalist*, *The Music Journal*, and *Music Educators Journal* (see Appendix A for a complete list of her written journal article publications). In addition to writing prose for the teaching of stringed instruments, she also wrote original compositions, including "Hohmann for the String Class" (1949), "Chatterbox Symphonette" (1950), and

Figure 2.15 Elizabeth Green, circa 1958.
Source: Elizabeth Green Papers, Bentley Historical Library, University of Michigan.

"12 Modern Etudes for the Advanced Violinist" (1964). Appendix B lists her publications related to stringed instruments.

Elizabeth believed that conductors should not only practice the gestures involved in leading a music ensemble, but also comprehensively study the music score. After their initial meeting in 1942, Elizabeth and Malko remained in contact, and Elizabeth took private conducting lessons to advance her conducting knowledge and movement skills. During the summer of 1947, Elizabeth and Malko communicated about writing a book. In a letter to her parents, dated July 3, 1947, Elizabeth mentioned mailing outlines of a conducting text to Malko for his approval. Alongside this statement, she remarked on locating a publisher for the text, stating that "university presses are not an option because they do not print music books and Presser is the best option."[86] Elizabeth also mentioned that she was learning Russian – a skill that would undoubtedly be useful for later publications.

In her career, Elizabeth published several books on the topic of conducting, including *The Modern Conductor* (1961, 1969, 1981, 1987, 1992, 1997, 2004), *The Conductor and His Score* (1976), and *The Dynamic Orchestra: Principles of Orchestral Performance for Instrumentalists, Conductors and Audiences* (1987). *The Modern Conductor* (currently in its seventh edition) is a seminal text on conducting technique and score study that is referenced and utilized in many undergraduate conducting courses. The book is inscribed as follows: "A college text on conducting based on the technical principles of Nicolai Malko as set forth in his *The Conductor and His Baton*" (1950).[87] Elizabeth studied conducting with Nicolai Malko[88] and crafted a text that merged Malko's principles of conductor movement and her understanding of brain research. Elizabeth wrote:

> Our hands will learn whatever we teach them. As our skills mature, the time ultimately arrives when our musical thoughts appear in our gestures, but only if the training has taken place. Practicing the exercises strengthens the "neural pathway" from brain to hands.[89]

To accompany this text, she created several exercises to assist in developing independent use of the hands.[90] While in Manchester during her sabbatical, Elizabeth found her book, *The Modern Conductor*, in the music shelves of the local library.

Malko passed away in 1961, but Malko's spouse and their son, George, continued to communicate with Elizabeth, not only as a way of preserving Malko's legacy but also because they had spent significant time together in Chicago over the years.[91] In 1964, Elizabeth was asked to rewrite and translate portions of Malko's last book, *A Certain Art*, and prepare it for publication.[92] The publication was released January 1, 1966.[93]

In *The Modern Conductor* (2004), Elizabeth wrote that "music lives only when the notes fly off the page and soar into glorious sound. The performer, the conductor, releases those notes from bondage through his or her feelings for the message through the power of imagination."[94] This quote embodies her philosophy of musical teaching and learning. As someone who was always learning, her vitality and spirit echo in this quote. More information about Elizabeth's teaching appears in Chapter 3; please refer to Appendix B for a bibliography of her publications related to conducting.

Figure 2.16 Elizabeth Green, circa 1950.
Source: Elizabeth Green Papers, Bentley Historical Library, University of Michigan.

Disseminating Knowledge Through Additional Teaching: Clinics and Workshops

Through her teaching career, Elizabeth maintained that a good music teacher was "dedicated to the musical ideal" and "dedicated to the student."[95] In this spirit, she began offering conducting workshops and clinics at conferences as early as her time in Waterloo, Iowa, in 1937.[96] Her expertise in string education was well known within the American String Teachers Association and she had presented at dozens of statewide, national, and international venues and organizations. Elizabeth's success as an in-service music teacher served as a solid foundation for continued work presenting sessions on string education for various music education organizations.[97] Her professional activity, including her adjudication experiences and guest conducting, was a complementary component of her career in music education.

Elizabeth was a prolific adjudicator and guest conductor at music festivals across the country, offering pedagogical comments to performing ensembles and soloists.[98] Upon inspecting her resume and list of professional engagements, it would be impossible to begin to list the breadth of her professional activity. Instead, I want to highlight a few prestigious professional engagements. In 1965, Elizabeth was invited to lecture at the Royal Danish Conservatory of Music in Copenhagen, Denmark, for the First Nicolai Malko (Memorial) International Competition for Young Conductors, and in 1971 and 1978, she returned as an adjudicator for the same event.[99] She traveled to about 25 states in the United States and Canada, serving in a similar role with many repeat engagements. This is an indication of Elizabeth's professionalism and preparation.

Service to the Profession

Elizabeth Green tirelessly served the music education through her professional appointments to national associations. In 1947, she was appointed vice-president of the North Central region (Michigan, Illinois, Indiana, and Ohio) and chairman of publicity for the American String Teachers Association (ASTA) under President Duane Haskill.[100] Her chairman of publicity position was critical in aiding with the dissemination of information and materials from national headquarters as well as for compiling mailing lists of interested prospective members.[101] During her time in leadership, membership grew, and by 1949, there were more than five hundred members.[102]

As the organization grew, Elizabeth served in other capacities within the organization. After relinquishing her two previous roles, she led the ASTA committee on Youth Orchestras (established in the 1960s).[103] Her important work on this committee led to the preparation of a document outlining *A Code of Ethics for School and Youth Orchestras*. The document included a statement that represents the essence of the committee's work:

> There is only one way to insure a musical future for the United States and that is to support the public school orchestral department. This

is where interest in created. This is where development progresses. This is what supplies the present-day private teacher with his heavy and remunerative schedule. This is what is keeping the college and university string departments alive. Without strings there is no orchestra. Without orchestra there is little or no real musical culture other than choral. The greatest musical literature is for the orchestra or the voice with orchestra. ... Youth orchestras must cooperate with the school orchestra director or else acknowledge that they are ultimately going to kill all orchestra participation in these United States.[104]

Retirement and Awards (1975–1995)

Elizabeth A. H. Green, Professor of Music, retired from active teaching status as of May 31, 1975, after a distinguished career as a musician, teacher, and author. In June 1975, Richard L. Kennedy (Secretary of the University of Michigan), wrote a report of Elizabeth's retirement, announcing: "The Regents salute this distinguished music educator for her dedicated service by naming her Professor Emeritus of Music."[105] During the next 20 years, Elizabeth continued to teach, learn, and share her love of music.

Retirement

In September 1974, Elizabeth began a year-long furlough prior to her full retirement in the spring of 1975.[106] In the summer 1974 issue of the *American String Teacher* journal, an article announced Elizabeth's retirement from the University of Michigan. It stated that "she estimates that she has taught well over 2,000 college students from 1955 ... and has guided many string players and conductors to successful positions." Reflecting on the quote from the first paragraph of Chapter 1 – "Where Elizabeth Green finds the time for all the activities in her busy life is somewhat of a mystery"[107] – it is clear that this continued into her retirement. Elizabeth Green spent her early retirement years completing several academic projects as well as exploring new areas of interest. One new area of interest was the visual arts, and Elizabeth took formal coursework at nearby Eastern Michigan University. Formalizing her plan to pursue visual art-making was something that she planned on for a few years preceding her retirement from the University of Michigan. In correspondence between Elizabeth, Kingsley Calkins (Head, Art Department), and Mead Hoover (Assistant Dean, Graduate School) between 1971 and 1973, she was admitted as a non-matriculating student.[108] In an interview

Figure 2.17 Elizabeth Green, circa 1974.
Source: Elizabeth Green Papers, Bentley Historical Library, University of Michigan.

conducted by Mary Damuth (Press Staff Writer, *Ann Arbor News*), Elizabeth mentioned why she would pursue her old dream.

> As a child, I loved to paint and draw, as all children do. But when you are in music, if you are taking it seriously, you do that. One art is enough. … As I visited arts shows around the state, Eastern Michigan inevitably came up because of their great art department. I wanted a good school because I was going to be serious.[109]

In 1978, she completed her Bachelor of Fine Arts (BFA) degree in painting and drawing. In addition to completing a BFA, Elizabeth was recommended to teach at the University of Michigan in immediate staffing situations, including in the fall term of 1981, when she was invited to teach a conducting course after the recent resignation of Assistant Professor Glenn Richter.[110]

Alongside exploring new areas of interest, Elizabeth Green updated and wrote new books about string instrument and conducting pedagogy,

Figure 2.18 Elizabeth Green's landscape pencil drawing.
Source: Used with permission by E. Daniel Long, circa 1976.

including *Orchestral Bowings and Routines* (1990) and *Miraculous Teacher: Ivan Galamian and the Meadowmount Experience* (published posthumously in 1996). She updated the third, fourth, and fifth editions of *The Modern Conductor* (1981, 1987, 1992). The main additions and modifications to these editions of this text were the inclusion of repertoire excerpts for classroom use, reordering Malko's training exercises, reorienting conducting as a "time-space art," and the addition of highlighted terminology to assist students retain vocabulary.[111] These modifications were significant to the book and allowed instructors of conducting to integrate this text without finding additional supplemental course materials. During the first two years of her retirement, Elizabeth was contacted by Nicolai Malko's widow and asked to complete his unfinished book, *The Conductor and His Score* (1976).

Elizabeth was authorized to use his notebook and to incorporate her own material.[112]

In her early retirement years, Elizabeth was dedicated to her studies in visual art at Eastern Michigan University. In 1980, she wrote a Christmas letter outlining her professional activities.

January	Third edition of *The Modern Conductor* sent to publisher
February	Six lectures for the Texas Music Educators
March	Judging competitions in Michigan
April	Represented Wheaton (Illinois) College at the Inauguration of the new President of the University of Michigan
May	Copenhagen, Denmark, for the Sixth Malko International Competition for Young Orchestra Conductors
June	One week of lectures on Conducting and Strings at Arizona State University, Tempe
July	My usual two-weeks Conducting Symposium at La Crosse, Wisconsin
August	Called back by University of Michigan to teach the Beginning Conducting classes for the school year 1980–1981
September	RETURN TO THE CLASSROOM! Six hours a week. Honored by the U of M Alumni Association (Music)
October	Two weekends lecturing: Winston-Salem, North Carolina, and Richmond, Virginia
November	Giving thanks for untold blessings
December	Conducting clinics and Strings: Michigan State University at East Lansing and at Grand Rapids[113]

During her later retirement years, Elizabeth received several invitations to appear and teach at conducting workshops. During the 1980s, she traveled to the University of Illinois (1986), as well as to Kitchener, Ontario (1988), and Milwaukee, Wisconsin (1998).[114] These presentations varied in topics from conducting fundamentals and score study to sessions about the brain and teaching philosophy.[115] One invitation was offered by Gary W. Hill, Director of Bands at the University of Missouri-Kansas City

Figure 2.19 Elizabeth Green holding her violin during retirement 1993.

and a former conducting student. Gary inquired if Elizabeth would be able to appear at an upcoming conducting workshop, but she declined.[116] One important local invitation was to guest conduct the University of Michigan Symphony Band in January 1984. Former student and Director of University Bands H. Robert Reynolds wrote "it meant so much to so many that you conducted. As I hope you could tell, the band thought that you were wonderful, and they are right, you are."[117] Around the same time, Elizabeth focused her time on book projects, including finishing her text, *The Dynamic Orchestra: Principles of Orchestral Performance for Instrumentalists, Conductors and Audiences* (1987), and *Practicing Successfully: A Masterclass in the Musical Art* (2006). At this point in her retirement, Elizabeth was more social, with a close group of friends, because she was no longer conducting or guest lecturing.[118]

Awards

Elizabeth was a decorated music educator and was honored by many music education organizations. In this section of the chapter, I will highlight a few of her accolades, with a full list of her awards appearing in Appendix C.

Elizabeth was well known, internationally, for her expertise on string instrument and conducting pedagogy, and her positive reputation in the music education field was recognized by the State of Michigan. In addition to her many local awards, Elizabeth was honored by the Michigan House of Representatives through receiving a citation.

Having extensively served the American String Teachers Association, in 1978, Elizabeth received the Distinguished Service Award. In the same year, she was honored by the Northwestern University Alumni Association and received the Distinguished Career Award. Almost two decades later, the American String Teachers Association named an award after Elizabeth, the Elizabeth A. H. Green School Educator Award, with E. Daniel Long, a string educator in Ann Arbor, as the first recipient in 1997.[119]

Elizabeth's reputation extended beyond the American String Teachers Association and to the esteemed American Bandmasters Association. In 1992, Robert Foster (President) wrote to Elizabeth, acknowledging that she was the recipient of the American Bandmasters Association Edwin Franko Goldman Memorial Citation.[120] This recognition is the highest honor that the American Bandmasters Association can bestow on a person outside their membership, for individuals who have promoted band music in America. In a letter acknowledging the receipt of her notification, Green wrote

> I cannot help but feel that my contribution to Bands is entirely due to the many fine students I have had over the years who have dedicated their lives to acquainting their students and audiences with the very best of the literature (music) for Band.[121]

Green's honorary society memberships include Phi Beta Mu, Pi Kappa Lambda, Delta Omicron, and Tau Beta Sigma.

In Memoriam

Elizabeth A. H. Green (1906–1995) – an internationally recognized music educator, conductor, and string performer – passed away on Sunday, September 24, 1995, at her home in Ann Arbor, Michigan, surrounded by friends and family.[122] Author of several music publications, Elizabeth Green began playing violin at a young age and continued playing until she was diagnosed with cancer in June 1995. After hearing her diagnosis, she refrained from receiving treatment in order to finish her last book, *Practicing Successfully: A Masterclass in the Musical Art* (2006), which was published posthumously years later.[123] Elizabeth guided many string players and conductors to successful careers, and her remarkable life and career in music education inspired thousands of her students. In 1942, she was appointed Assistant Professor of Music Education at the University of Michigan. In 1975, she retired from U-M as professor emerita and pursued studies in visual art at Eastern Michigan University, earning a second bachelor's in 1978 (see Appendix E for her obituary).

One of Elizabeth's former students, Robert Phillips, discussed details about her funeral, which occurred on Wednesday, September 27, 1995 at First Presbyterian Church (1432 Washtenaw Ave., Ann Arbor, Michigan). Phillips stated

> there was a group of teachers [former students] locally in Ann Arbor and we played at her funeral. This is a touching story. We played, I think, the Bach *Air on the G String* at her funeral. We played it without a conductor. Charlie Avsharian was the concert-master, a former student and owner of SHAR Music. ... The idea was that Elizabeth was conducting us. ... It was very touching.[124]

Another former student, Kevin Miller, remarked "it was one of the greatest outpourings of love for a former teacher I've ever witnessed. There were a number of people that spoke and it was such a great testimony to her."[125] Elizabeth was quoted as saying "I worry about them [her students]. My mother used to tell me I'd be a lot better off if I didn't 'adopt' every student I had."[126] This quote is prophetic of the upcoming chapters, which outline her pedagogy and relational capacity.

Notes

1 Elizabeth A. H. Green, "Then and Now," *American String Teacher* 27, no. 2 (Spring 1977): 14.
2 Green interview, March 11, 1985, quoted in Deborah Annette Smith, "Elizabeth A. H. Green: A Biography," Ph.D. diss., University of Michigan, Ann Arbor, 1986, ProQuest Dissertations and Theses Global (UMI No. 8621380): 71.
3 Ibid.
4 Smith, "Elizabeth A. H. Green: A Biography," 73; see page 67 of Ann Arbor High School Yearbook for confirmation of only 13 students enrolled in Spring 1942: https://aadl.org/sites/default/files/archives/yearbooks/yearbook-ann_arbor_high_school-1942.pdf. Consequently, there were only nine students enrolled in the 1941 Yearbook: https://aadl.org/sites/default/files/archives/yearbooks/yearbook-ann_arbor_high_school-1941.pdf.
5 Verne Edman Collins, "Music in Ann Arbor High School," Ed.D. diss., University of Michigan, Ann Arbor, 1966, ProQuest Dissertations and Theses Global (UMI No. 6701718): 236.
6 Folder 16, Correspondence 1942, Bulletins, Box 2, Folder 16. Elizabeth Green Papers, SC-032. Buswell Library Special Collections.

7   Ibid.
8   See pp. 44–45 of Ann Arbor High School 1943 Yearbook, https://aadl.org/sites/default/files/archives/yearbooks/yearbook-ann_arbor_high_school-1943.pdf.
9   Collins, "Music in Ann Arbor High School," 234–235; See p. 84 of Ann Arbor High School 1944 Yearbook, https://aadl.org/sites/default/files/archives/yearbooks/yearbook-ann_arbor_high_school-1944.pdf.
10 See page 35 of Ann Arbor High School 1945 Yearbook, https://aadl.org/sites/default/files/archives/yearbooks/yearbook-ann_arbor_high_school-1945.pdf.
11 Ibid., 82.
12 Green interview, March 18, 1985, quoted in Smith, 83.
13 Smith, "Elizabeth A. H. Green: A Biography," 83.
14 Ibid.
15 Green interview, March 18, 1985, quoted in Smith, 84.
16 Folder 18, Correspondence 1942, Bulletins, Box 2, Folder 18. Elizabeth Green Papers, SC-032. Buswell Library Special Collections.
17 Folder 17, Correspondence 1942, Bulletins, Box 2, Folder 17. Elizabeth Green Papers, SC-032. Buswell Library Special Collections.
18 Smith, "Elizabeth A. H. Green: A Biography," 78.
19 Ibid., 80.
20 Ibid.
21 Folder 13, Contract Correspondence, Bulletins, Box 5, Folder 13. Elizabeth Green Papers, SC-032. Buswell Library Special Collections.
22 Smith, "Elizabeth A. H. Green: A Biography," 85.
23 Folder 18, Correspondence November 1942, Bulletins, Box 2, Folder 18. Elizabeth Green Papers, SC-032. Buswell Library Special Collections.
24 Folder 16, Correspondence 1942, Bulletins, Box 2, Folder 16. Elizabeth Green Papers, SC-032. Buswell Library Special Collections.
25 Executive Committee Meeting Minutes, June 17, 1942, School of Music Records, Box 52, Folder 9, University of Michigan Archives, Ann Arbor; Shelley C. Cooper, "Marguerite Vivian Hood (1903–1992): Her Life and Contributions to Music Education," Ph.D. diss., Arizona State University, Tempe, 2004, ProQuest Dissertations and Theses Global (UMI No. 3123530), 127.
26 Proceedings of the Board of Regents, October Meeting 1942, University of Michigan, Ann Arbor, 83.
27 Smith, 98; Green interview, March 18, 1985.
28 Folder 13, Contract Correspondence, Bulletins, Box 5, Folder 13. Elizabeth Green Papers, SC-032. Buswell Library Special Collections.
29 Smith, "Elizabeth A. H. Green: A Biography," 89–91.
30 Ibid., 92.
31 Ibid.
32 Green interview, March 18, 1985, quoted in Smith, 92.
33 Merle Jay Hansen, "David Earl Mattern: A Biography," Ph.D., diss., University of Michigan, Ann Arbor, 1974, ProQuest Dissertations and Theses Global (UMI No. 7510181), 173.

34 Smith, "Elizabeth A. H. Green: A Biography," 106.
35 Proceedings of the Board of Regents, September Meeting 1957, University of Michigan, Ann Arbor, 145.
36 Smith, "Elizabeth A. H. Green: A Biography," 111.
37 Hansen, "David Earl Mattern: A Biography," 178.
38 Smith, "Elizabeth A. H. Green: A Biography," 112. The University Elementary School was a laboratory school affiliated with the University of Michigan and established in 1930.
39 Executive Committee Meeting Minutes, October 21, 1960, School of Music Records, Box 52, Folder 10, University of Michigan Archives, Ann Arbor.
40 Smith, "Elizabeth A. H. Green: A Biography," 113.
41 Proceedings of the Board of Regents, May Meeting 1963, University of Michigan, Ann Arbor, 1172.
42 Smith, "Elizabeth A. H. Green: A Biography," 113.
43 Folder 5, Correspondence – Green, Elizabeth, 1951–1991, Box 38, Folder 5. Allen Perdue Britton Papers, 0135-SCPA. Michelle Smith Performing Arts Library Special Collections.
44 Ibid.
45 Smith, "Elizabeth A. H. Green: A Biography," 114.
46 Folder 5, Correspondence – Green, Elizabeth, 1951–1991, Box 38, Folder 5. Allen Perdue Britton Papers, 0135-SCPA. Michelle Smith Performing Arts Library Special Collections.
47 Ibid.
48 Smith, "Elizabeth A. H. Green: A Biography," 115; "Standard Practice Guide Policies: Retirement Furlough No. 201.81," University of Michigan, last modified January 12, 2001, https://spg.umich.edu/policy/201.81.
49 Folder 16, Correspondence 1942, Bulletins, Box 2, Folder 16. Elizabeth Green Papers, SC-032. Buswell Library Special Collections.
50 Ibid.
51 Elizabeth A. H. Green, "Obituary," *Detroit Free Press* (Detroit, Michigan), September 26, 1995.
52 Ibid.
53 Folder 29, Correspondence 1953, Bulletins, Box 2, Folder 29. Elizabeth Green Papers, SC-032. Buswell Library Special Collections.
54 Frances Jordan McHugh, "Crowd Cheers Miss Green's Violin Solo," *Waterloo Courier*, n.d.
55 Smith, "Elizabeth A. H. Green: A Biography," 128.
56 Green interview, April 2, 1985, quoted in Smith, 128.
57 Folder 17, Correspondence 1941, Bulletins, Box 2, Folder 17. Elizabeth Green Papers, SC-032. Buswell Library Special Collections.
58 Ibid.
59 Smith, 129.
60 Green interview, April 2, 1985, quoted in Smith, 129.
61 Folder 18, Correspondence 1942, Bulletins, Box 2, Folder 18. Elizabeth Green Papers, SC-032. Buswell Library Special Collections.
62 Green interview, April 2, 1985, quoted in Smith, 129.

63 Folder 20, Correspondence 1944, Bulletins, Box 2, Folder 20. Elizabeth Green Papers, SC-032. Buswell Library Special Collections.

64 Folder 23, Correspondence 1947, Bulletins, Box 2, Folder 23. Elizabeth Green Papers, SC-032. Buswell Library Special Collections.

65 Folder 31, Correspondence 1964, Bulletins, Box 2, Folder 31. Elizabeth Green Papers, SC-032. Buswell Library Special Collections.

66 Ibid.

67 Folder 5, Correspondence – Green, Elizabeth, 1951–1991, Box 38, Folder 5. Allen Perdue Britton Papers, 0135-SCPA. Michelle Smith Performing Arts Library Special Collections.

68 Folder 31, Correspondence 1964, Bulletins, Box 2, Folder 31. Elizabeth Green Papers, SC-032. Buswell Library Special Collections

69 *Interlochen Bowl*, souvenir edition (Ann Arbor: National Music Camp, 1943): 4, 8.

70 Smith, "Elizabeth A. H. Green: A Biography," 100–101.

71 Executive Committee Meeting Minutes, April 20, 1948, School of Music Records, Box 52, Folder 10, University of Michigan Archives, Ann Arbor; Proceedings of the Board of Regents, July Meeting 1948, University of Michigan, Ann Arbor, 36.

72 Folder 23, Correspondence 1947, Bulletins, Box 2, Folder 23. Elizabeth Green Papers, SC-032. Buswell Library Special Collections.

73 Ibid.

74 Ibid.

75 Folder 24, Correspondence 1948, Bulletins, Box 2, Folder 24. Elizabeth Green Papers, SC-032. Buswell Library Special Collections.

76 Elizabeth A. H. Green, "Group Conducting," September 20, 1978, University of Connecticut, reel-to-reel converted to mp3, Box 1. Elizabeth Green Papers, Bentley Historical Library, University of Michigan; Elizabeth A. H. Green, "Lecture," September 20, 1978, University of Connecticut, reel-to-reel converted to mp3, Box 1. Elizabeth Green Papers, Bentley Historical Library, University of Michigan.

77 Folder 15, Correspondence 1941, Bulletins, Box 2, Folder 15. Elizabeth Green Papers, SC-032. Buswell Library Special Collections.

78 "Prof. Green to Conduct Indiana Orchestra Contest," *Ann Arbor News*, October 19, 1948; "Prof. Green to Direct Virginia Student Orchestra," *Ann Arbor News*, November 30, 1948.

79 Folder 24, Correspondence 1948, Bulletins, Box 2, Folder 24. Elizabeth Green Papers, SC-032. Buswell Library Special Collections.

80 Folder 23, Correspondence 1947, Bulletins, Box 2, Folder 23. Elizabeth Green Papers, SC-032. Buswell Library Special Collections.

81 Folder 24, Correspondence 1948, Bulletins, Box 2, Folder 24. Elizabeth Green Papers, SC-032. Buswell Library Special Collections.

82 Ibid.

83 Ibid.

84 Ibid.

85 Folder 26, Correspondence 1950, Bulletins, Box 2, Folder 26. Elizabeth Green Papers, SC-032. Buswell Library Special Collections.

86 Folder 23, Correspondence 1947, Bulletins, Box 2, Folder 23. Elizabeth Green Papers, SC-032. Buswell Library Special Collections.

87 Nicolai Malko, *The Conductor and His Baton: Fundamentals of the Technique of Conducting* (Wilhelm Hansen, 1950).

88 Nicolai Malko, the great Russian conductor, developed his analyses of conducting gestures during his years as Administrative Director and Chief Conductor of the Leningrad Philharmonic Orchestra and concurrently as Professor of Conducting and Chairman of the Conducting Department at the Glinka Conservatory of Music in Leningrad.

89 Green, *The Modern Conductor*, xiii.

90 Elizabeth A. Green, "Malko Conducting Exercises," *YouTube*, 25:57, February 8, 2017, www.youtube.com/watch?v=oZYFi89Ph4g.

91 Folder 31, Correspondence 1964, Bulletins, Box 2, Folder 31. Elizabeth Green Papers, SC-032. Buswell Library Special Collections.

92 Ibid.

93 Nicoli A. Malko, *A Certain Art* (New York: William Morrow, 1966); Néstor Castiglione, "George Malko on the Life and 'Certain Art' of His Father Nicoli," last modified April 6, 2021, www.echorrhea.com/interviews/malko-on-malko.

94 Elizabeth A. Green and Mark Gibson, *The Modern Conductor* (Upper Saddle River, NJ: Prentice Hall, 2004), xv.

95 Ibid.

96 Smith, "Elizabeth A. H. Green: A Biography," 116; Folder 31, General 1937, Bulletins, Box 4, Folder 31. Elizabeth Green Papers, SC-032. Buswell Library Special Collections.

97 Ibid.

98 Ibid.

99 Smith, 117.

100 Robert Allen Ritsema, "A History of the American String Teachers Association: The First Twenty-Five Years," Ed.D. diss., University of Michigan, Ann Arbor, 1971), ProQuest Dissertations and Theses Global (UMI No. 7214777): 33–34.

101 Ibid., 28–31.

102 Ibid., 39–40.

103 Smith, 90.

104 Elizabeth A. H. Green, "An Open Letter to All Conductors of Youth Orchestras," *American String Teacher* 14, no. 4 (1964): 13.

105 Report of Faculty Retirement, June 1975, News and Information Services, Box 5, Folder 6, University of Michigan Archives, Ann Arbor.

106 News Release, June 1975, News and Information Services, Box 5, Folder 6, University of Michigan Archives, Ann Arbor.

107 This statement was included in an editor's note for Elizabeth Green's journal article, "Three Works I Would Hate to Teach Without," *Repertoire* 1, no. 1 (1951): 45.

108 Folder 36, Correspondence 1971, Bulletins, Box 2, Folder 36. Elizabeth Green Papers, SC-032. Buswell Library Special Collections.

109 "Music Prof Turned Art Student," *Ann Arbor News*, May 7, 1978.

110 Faculty Appointment Recommendation, August 1981, News and Information Services, Box 5, Folder 8, University of Michigan Archives, Ann Arbor.

111 Elizabeth A. H. Green, *The Modern Conductor* (Englewood Cliffs, NJ: Prentice Hall, 1992): vii.

112 Elizabeth A. H. Green, n.d., School of Music Records, Box 2, Folder 1, University of Michigan Archives, Ann Arbor.

113 Folder 38, Correspondence 1980s, Bulletins, Box 2, Folder 38. Elizabeth Green Papers, SC-032. Buswell Library Special Collections.

114 Personal Materials, Box 1, Elizabeth Green Papers, Bentley Historical Library, University of Michigan.

115 Ibid.

116 Gary Hill to Elizabeth Green, September 10, 1986.

117 H. Robert Reynolds to Elizabeth Green, January 25, 1984.

118 Long interview, October 4, 2017.

119 Jared R. Rawlings, "'Don't Keep It a Secret': E. Daniel Long and His Career in Music Education," *Journal of Historical Research in Music Education* 42, no. 2 (2021): 159–179.

120 Folder 39, Correspondence 1990s, Bulletins, Box 2, Folder 39. Elizabeth Green Papers, SC-032. Buswell Library Special Collections.

121 Ibid.

122 Green's residence: 1225 Ferdon Road, Ann Arbor, MI, 48104; Joshua Feigelson, "Elizabeth A. H. Green 1906–1995," *American String Teacher* 45, no. 4 (1995): 21.

123 Feigelson, 21.

124 Phillips interview, March 7, 2018.

125 Miller interview, May 18, 2018.

126 Report of Faculty Retirement, July 1974, News and Information Services, Box 5, Folder 8, University of Michigan Archives, Ann Arbor.

3 The Pedagogical Philosophy of Elizabeth A. H. Green

"How to Make Your Flowers Grow"

Regardless of the level of student you teach, you must be a top musician and performer yourself. To teach a beginner well, the teacher should also be at home in the top-level music performance. You can't teach what you don't know yourself.[1]

– Elizabeth A. H. Green

Training instrumental music teachers to teach large ensembles is complex work and often requires the intentional merger of instrumental music knowledge and skill of conducting gesture during preservice music teacher education coursework.[2] Elizabeth A. H. Green was a pioneer in the field of instrumental music teacher education, as she was one of the first teachers to struggle with and document this complex work in the form of a curriculum for teaching conducting.[3] Moreover, she was a dedicated string pedagogue and codified string teaching techniques that influenced generations of instrumental music teachers and teacher educators.

The first two chapters of this book presented a biographical representation of Elizabeth A. H. Green's life and career in music education. Based on these biographical details, Elizabeth's strong reputation as a leader in the fields of conducting and string performance makes her a unique figure in music education history, and an examination of her teaching philosophy is needed to uncover details of her motivations, strongly held core beliefs about music, and instructional values. Within this chapter, I will share selected quotes of interview data assembled from her past students, friends, and colleagues.[4] In the first section of the chapter, I present Elizabeth's teaching philosophy as it relates to conducting and string pedagogy. In the second section of this chapter, I present how Elizabeth used her diagnostic skill as formative assessment toward a systematic way of learning and knowing. In the final section

DOI: 10.4324/9781003152415-3

of this chapter, I present evidence about how Elizabeth made clear her commitment to affective fulfillment and the use of imagination.

Elizabeth A. H. Green's Teaching Philosophy

Elizabeth A. H. Green has been described by many as an innovator who revolutionized the way conducting and string pedagogy was and still remains conceptualized and taught. Moreover, her legacy as an instrumental music teacher educator reverberates through not only her writings, but also the stories and memories of her teaching. Her educational purpose and learning goals have remained somewhat of a mystery; however, within this section of the chapter, I will present details of her motivations, strongly held core beliefs about music, and instructional values.

Content Mastery and Musicianship Through Experiential Learning

Elizabeth A. H. Green considered one end goal or purpose of education to be musicianship through experiential learning. As the quote opening this chapter suggests, she believed that all music teachers needed to be strong performers or master musicians. In asking some of the informants about what they remembered with regard to her university conducting class, former student Robert Jager shared a vivid memory. He stated:

> It [the class] always began with a little bit of exercise. I remember one of the things we always did was that we immediately had to stand and it's something you just did after we got used to the procedures. We would stand up and then she would start talking about the topic for the day ... she might say something like active versus passive gestures. ... She would have a routine that she'd go through. Then there were things like "keep your wrist free from your lower arm and keep it flexible." You raise your arm up and you drop your hand then you reverse it, raise your hand and drop your arm and sideways and you do all of these things and get your arm muscles in shape. ... Almost every class began with that kind of thing. Another one was a gesture of syncopation. She would say something like, "Syncopation on two." You knew that when you got to the second beat, you'd bounce it. On four, bounce it on four. She had these imbedded in the class, that routine. Then, after we did that for probably five or ten minutes, we'd go into the lesson of the day.[5]

In addition to this scaffolded approach to lessons, Elizabeth taught her students how to internalize music notation as a way of preparing for rehearsing and teaching. Bob Phillips, a former student and retired public school music educator, remarked:

> She had you write the themes and the number of measures out in note cards. I remember one of the pieces that I worked on memorizing was Brandenburg No. 4, 1st movement. Her process was that you would write out on note cards for every eight bars (the length of a phrase) thematic analysis – it was a little like Schenkerian analysis. You started at the micro-level and you worked backwards to the macro-level. Next week, you would write it out for 16-bar phrases, then you'd write for 32-bar, etc. By the time you got all done, you had one card that said Brandenburg concerto No. 4, movement 1. It might just say ABA or what the form was or whatever, but she had you work from small phrases to bigger phrases, to even bigger phrases, to biggest phrases. She had you write down the conducting gestures too like what needed to be cued, that kind of thing. It wasn't memorizing the notes as much as it was memorizing

Figure 3.1 Elizabeth Green leading a conducting class at Interlochen Music
Camp, circa 1945.

Source: Used with permission by E. Daniel Long.

the form and where all the important cues were, that kind of thing. We also had to write all the harmonic structure. You'd know for eight bars, here's the chord sequence, here's the harmonic flow. Eventually, you've got one card that says D major, etc. That's how I remember it.[6]

Robert Haskell argued that teacher educators must adopt a spiral approach in which concepts and skills are constantly revisited, reinforced, and applied within different examples.[7] Moreover, Haskell stressed the significance of teaching students where and how the subject content fits into the larger curricular sequence. This scaffolding approach is not linear; rather, it is a fluid process, regularly referring to previous learning while looking ahead to new examples, contexts, and scenarios. In order to teach music skill acquisition in this manner, music teacher educators must be proficient in transfer of thinking, and it seems as though Elizabeth Green was particularly skilled at this concept.

Music teachers need to be strong performers, and Elizabeth would model the dedicated behaviors it took to reach this goal, including being organized. This principle of her teaching philosophy was reflected in her elementary and secondary teaching. From the start of her years teaching orchestra classes with Ann Arbor Public Schools (1942–1953), Elizabeth was dedicated to music performance. Alice Sano, a former Ann Arbor High School Orchestra cellist (1942–1946), remarked

> when she was with elementary school students, Miss Green carried all of these violins in the car. Students didn't keep them in those days ... carried them in a car and carried to the class. She was so dedicated and wanted her students to have a good experience.[8]

Along this theme of dedication, Elizabeth impressed her value of strong musicianship on her college students as well. Barbara Barstow, a former student of Elizabeth's, remembered:

> Rehearse with the utmost professionalism. I do believe that because of the way Elizabeth taught me. I treated my adult orchestra just like the kids. They're all musicians and you respect them on the podium and you give them your all. You teach and you study and you work hard at your score and learn your parts, your transposition ... Elizabeth was so knowledgeable on every point. And I was so impressed with the knowledge she had.[9]

Figure 3.2 Elizabeth Green playing violin, circa 1965.
Source: Used with permission by MLive Media Group.

Elizabeth was exceptionally organized and valued mentoring her university preservice music teachers. Larry Livingston, a former student of Elizabeth, said,

> I saw her as incredibly well organized, very thoughtful teacher with a very specific pedagogy. Her relationship with her students was very much teacher/mentor student, not friend although she was not a tyrant of any kind.[10]

Elizabeth encouraged all aspiring music teachers to take her classes. E. Daniel Long remarked that

> When you went into her studio, her violin class, her conducting class, it was filled with choir, orchestra, band people. She didn't care. ... You were looked upon as someone who taught music, through various different mediums. ... But, that was an important part of her philosophical beliefs, that she looked upon you, everybody was

looked upon as being the same. You were all had the potential of being this great teacher and she was going to help you find your avenue on how best to do it.[11]

One of the hallmarks of Elizabeth's pedagogy was her commitment to experiential learning. She believed that students needed to make music rather than being told about it. A former student and retired Professor Emeritus (Director of Bands) from the University of Michigan, H. Robert Reynolds, discussed her value of musicianship, stating,

> She could do everything she was asking us to do … she had specific outlines and was extremely organized. Miss Green was also flexible and departed from her lesson when she needed to correct us in violin class. The conducting classes, after she instructed us on the basic things, she would then give us short examples as assignments so we could work on the concept.[12]

Another example along this theme was Elizabeth's belief that her student's conducting needed to be clear. Kevin Miller, a former student and retired Director of Orchestral Activities at Eastern Michigan University, remarked:

> I would say what I appreciate most from her conducting pedagogy was the emphasis on clarity in conducting. When I'm a player in an ensemble, what I appreciate the most is if the conductor is clear. I have been complimented many times over the years from players who like the fact they can follow what I am doing. That they can see where the down beat is and I attribute a lot of that to what she advocates in her textbook – being clear. I mean something as simple as not letting the rebound of the down beat be higher than half the distance of the from the top of the down beat to down to the bottom, so that the other beats don't get confused with down beats. Little things like that, but I think especially when you're conducting an ensemble for the first time where you have only one rehearsal with them. Being clear is so important.[13]

Elizabeth's ability to model performing skills for her students was ahead of its time. Modeling a skill was a commonly mentioned pedagogy among the informants. Such an approach is sometimes informally referred to as *I do–We do–You do*, and this pedagogical strategy is utilized to ensure a "gradual release of responsibility."[14] In other words, the process itself is differentiated in that it works through three tiers that challenge students.

Elizabeth's ability to model the skills she was asking her students to demonstrate is no small task and is preceded by hours of preparation. Judith Palac, retired Professor Emerita (String Music Education) from Michigan State University, recalled that

> she did not like the tone that the bass player was pulling. She said, "You're such a big guy. You can pull a bigger tone than that." He tried and wasn't doing it. He tried again and wasn't doing it. She walked back there, because he was in the back of the class and she takes that three-quarters sized bass, tips it towards her and put that German bow on the bass. The sound shook the rafters. It was like everybody jumped back. Here she was, 80 something years old, four feet, eight inches tall and she could still pull the tone out of a bass like you couldn't believe. It so shows how impassioned she was. At this age, why should she care if this kid could pull a tone out of the bass? She just would not let that go.[15]

Much of Elizabeth's life was dedicated to ensuring that her students mastered their content, and it seems that she would leave no stone unturned to help her students. E. Daniel Long, a retired AAPS instrumental music teacher and long-time friend of Elizabeth, remembered Elizabeth telling him a story about her teaching years in Waterloo, Iowa.

> In the summer time, she would go to some of these little towns in the Midwest and there would be the local band playing in the park. When she stopped to listen, she noticed there was a problem with two or three of those bands, and it was a recurring problem. She thought, "I think there's a solution. What was the problem?" The problem was they had no French horn players. So, she went home, gets a brass pedagogy book, a method book on how to play the French horn, and she sat down and she taught herself how to play French horn. Then she joined these little local summer bands, around Waterloo, and she would play French horn, in the band.[16]

Diagnosis and Formative Assessment as Systematic Learning

Throughout the cognitive interview process, a prominent impression was shared and voiced among the informants – Elizabeth Green was an incredibly accurate *diagnostician*. E. Daniel Long remarked:

She was a very perceptive person. She could analyze, on the spot, things that needed to be fixed, whether it be in someone's playing or someone's conducting. She was really great at analyzing. That's what made her unique, I think ... one of the great music educators and pedagogues of our time. The fact was that she had the ability to figure out what needed to be done. The devil was in the detail. She would spend hours focusing ... she just never gave up to try to help her students. It's as if her time wasn't important to her, just so long as she was helping her students.[17]

From her perspicacious perception to systematic instruction, Elizabeth was also known for her ability to explain abstract concepts in concrete, simplified statements. Robert Jager mentioned that "Miss Green was a master at simplifying instruction ... she doesn't let the material get in the way of the instruction."[18] E. Daniel Long extended this sentiment by adding, "she had a strategy, to how she diagnosed. She'd look at your right hand and she looked at the left hand ... movement and playing issues."[19] Through her accurate diagnosis of movement and playing issues, Elizabeth was modeling to her students what good teaching looked like. Larry Livingston, remarked that "we saw from the first day ... a very, very systematic way of doing everything; how you stand, how you hold the baton, how you cue, how you beat time patterns ... this was essential for modeling good teaching."[20] Reflecting back on her university classes, Larry Hurst, a former student and colleague of Elizabeth Green, said:

I remember one thing she used to do that I incorporate to this day. It is introducing the bow to the kids. You know there's a lot of playing open strings pizzicato, then ultimately, the bow is placed in the hands and they have to deal with where the fingers go. She had the kids extend their arms and just turn their hands over the thumbs to the right. So that simple kind of a *no frills* approach was so respected and it saved enormous amounts of time. That was her credo. If you can do it in two minutes, get it down to one minute with her. ... She would also use us as guinea pigs, of sorts, and use our mistakes as moments for group-level correction and it was very effective because she really wanted us all to do well. She gave feedback in such a way that no one was humiliated or felt lesser of a person because they couldn't demonstrate a skill. That was her trademark. She had a way of breaking down instruction to its simplest form. It wasn't dumbed down.[21]

Contributing to her accuracy of diagnosing errors was how she went about correcting her students' skill demonstration. Kevin Miller remarked that "she was one of those people that could speak very directly, but was always very kind."[22] Bob Phillips remembered a similar experience:

> She was kind but professional. She told them exactly what was right or wrong, what went well, what didn't go well, but it was at all times focused on the outcome. It was never personal. For example, I remember her saying this "This is what your stick is doing, this is what it's not doing. This is what your eyes are doing," that kind of thing ... she could look at you and see exactly where the mechanical flaws were.[23]

With both humility and confidence, Elizabeth would take opportunities to give credit where credit was due. For instance, informants mentioned that she would tell them when she was demonstrating techniques from her conducting and/or string teachers. Barbara Barstow said, "she taught us the most precise way of conducting with all the tools ... she took no credit and it was always Nicolai Malko that gave her all of this and it wasn't her ... but it was her."[24] After explaining further, Barstow observed that Elizabeth's way of teaching a skill, attributed to Nicolai Malko, was unique to her. The explanation of a skill was Elizabeth's creative contribution to our field.

Affective Fulfillment and Imagination

One trademark of Elizabeth A. H. Green was her imagination and ability to inspire her many students over the years to use theirs when studying and teaching music. One resounding theme from the interviews was her advocacy for every rehearsal to include at least one musical moment that resulted in affective fulfillment. Judith Palac and E. Daniel Long made clear in their interviews that "Elizabeth Green's goal was always to try to achieve that musical moment. Every tool, every mechanism, every imagination, every part of your existence, that was our job."[25] This goal is challenging, especially given all of the requirements and stressors placed on music teachers. One unique complexity of this goal is understanding that a musical moment is different for everyone. E. Daniel Long stated:

> You had to have figure out ways to get musical moments to happen. Now, sometimes it was little hard and I always worked toward that goal. I have always remembered that. Every time I'd walk into a rehearsal room and then getting ready for the next rehearsal. Sometimes consciously and sometimes unconsciously ... where's

the musical moment going to be? A musical moment is different for everybody.[26]

He went on to emphasize that the goal of teaching music was exactly, that – teaching music. It was not about teaching the notation; it was

> teaching music beyond notation and she spent a lot of time doing research on how the brain works. And then, teaching you, through your brain ... she talked about imagination all the time. Using your imagination as a music teacher.[27]

Conclusion

To Elizabeth A. H. Green, teaching music was about the art of music making. She wholeheartedly believed that to be a great music teacher, you had to be a great musician, regardless of your medium. Her teaching philosophy influenced decades of music teachers around the world, and she left no stone unturned to help her students. E. Daniel Long said: "Time was not important to her. What was important to her was getting it done right."[28] She would work tirelessly to be prepared, organized, and thoughtful in her musical leadership. During her tenure at the University of Michigan, she served two departments: Music Education and Strings. Larry Hurst remarked, "I saw Elizabeth a lot, even as a student ... she was very dedicated. ... Elizabeth had the respect of both departments and that's really a tough order ... it was unique and in those days was practically unheard of."[29]

Notes

1 Green interview, March 19, 1985 quoted in Deborah Annette Smith, "Elizabeth A. H. Green: A Biography," Ph.D. diss., University of Michigan, Ann Arbor, 1986, ProQuest Dissertations and Theses Global (UMI No. 8621380).
2 Sommer H. Forrester, "Music Teacher Knowledge: An Examination of the Intersections Between Instrumental Music Teaching and Conducting," Ph.D. diss., University of Michigan, Ann Arbor, 2015, ProQuest Dissertations and Theses Global (UMI No. 3731290).
3 Ibid.
4 Details of the informants can be found within the Acknowledgments and the interview methodology can be found in the Appendix section of this book.
5 Jager interview, October 4, 2018.
6 Phillips interview, March 7, 2018.
7 Robert E. Haskell, *Transfer of Learning: Cognition and Instruction* (Elsevier, 2000).

8   Sano interview, March 8, 2018.
9   Barstow interview, May 21, 2018.
10 Livingston interview, April 2, 2021.
11 Long interview, September 28, 2017.
12 Reynolds interview, October 9, 2017.
13 Miller interview, March 2, 2019.
14 Jerome S. Bruner, *The Process of Education* (Harvard University Press, 2009).
15 Palac interview, August 4, 2018.
16 Long interview, September 28, 2017.
17 Ibid.
18 Jager interview, October 4, 2018.
19 Long interview, October 3, 2017.
20 Livingston interview, April 2, 2021.
21 Hurst interview, May 20, 2018.
22 Miller interview, March 2, 2019.
23 Phillips interview, March 7, 2018.
24 Barstow interview, May 21, 2018.
25 Long interview, October 4, 2017.
26 Ibid.
27 Ibid.
28 Long interview, September 28, 2017.
29 Hurst interview, May 20, 2018.

4 Relational Trust and a Capacity to Influence Others

An atmosphere of trust, love, and humor can nourish extraordinary human capacity.

– Marilyn Ferguson, *The Aquarian Conspiracy* (1987)

Teacher education scholars are fascinated with codifying "What makes a good teacher?" For decades, these scholars have argued that teaching and learning depend fundamentally on the quality of relationships between teachers and students. During the 1930s and 1940s, A. S. Barr and his graduate students at the University of Wisconsin conducted dozens of studies examining characteristics of good teaching.[1] They studied teachers across grade levels and disciplines and identified many personal and professional characteristics of exceptional teachers. Toward the end of these investigations, Barr questioned whether there were universal pedagogical qualities of exceptional teachers that could predict success in teaching across all grade levels and disciplines.

It may be that there are universal pedagogical qualities of exceptional teachers; however, looking at qualities in individuals fails to capture the unique dynamic of teachers engaging with students in context. There is little research about how music teachers develop relationships with students or how music teacher education prepares future and in-service teachers to do this work. This chapter is dedicated to presenting information-rich descriptions of Elizabeth Green's tremendous capacity for building relationships with her students and colleagues during a life and career in music education. One approach to framing these descriptions is to contextualize and view them through a conceptual framework. One such conceptual framework is *relational capacity*. Relational capacity describes the teacher's ability to relate to the students in their classroom and includes interpersonal skills, such as humor, rapport, understanding, empathy, patience, respect, and trust.[2]

DOI: 10.4324/9781003152415-4

Articulating the relational practices of teaching is arguably critical for those aiming to prepare teachers.

Green's Presence in Teaching

Those who worked with Elizabeth Green describe her *presence in teaching* as unforgettable. Education scholars define presence as

> a state of alert awareness, receptivity, and connectedness to the mental, emotional, and physical workings of both the individual and the group in the context of their learning environments, and the ability to respond with a considered and compassionate best next step.[3]

The concept of *presence in music teaching* is a relatively new concept being examined within the field of music education; Shannan Hibbard argues that "the need to understand the role of the music teacher in relationship to students in situated contexts is one that is important than ever."[4]

Several interviewees described elements of teacher presence demonstrating Green's relational capacity. Throughout the interviews, the informants prominently described the classroom environment. E. Daniel (Dan) Long, a close friend of Elizabeth and an Ann Arbor music teacher, remembered that

> she would create an environment encouraging a desire to learn. Whether she was lecturing to a room full of people, at a convention, or just you, in her living room. ... There was an atmosphere of her showing, in various different ways, how she truly wanted to make music be a part of everybody's life in some way, as a teacher. She would just continually speak about how to deal with that. I mean, how to approach the left hand, or the right hand, or how to approach vibrato, or how to approach sighting, or how to approach all kinds of other things, or how to approach to get kids to use their imagination.[5]

Dan also mentioned that "she could make you feel like you were the only student in the room,"[6] that it was "the way she would speak. The way she would look at you ... the way she would respond to questions."[7] He went on to describe a memory when he and Elizabeth worked on a music excerpt together:

> I will never forget the time ... I had some particular issue and I called her up and I said, "Ms. Green, I have this problem and

I would like to have some help on it." And she said, "Good, come over next Tuesday at 4:00." Alright, that meant 3:45 to me. So, that memory is a way of describing how there was something special about her. You did not want to disappoint her. You made sure that you did not want to be late in this case. You always knew that 4:00 mean 3:45 and she was ready at 3:45. You just knew that, even when it came to such things as a time, you did not want to be late. So, off I went …

Although Dan was never her student in an official role, Elizabeth offered to talk about music whenever he wanted.

H. Robert Reynolds, a former student of Elizabeth's, described her presence as empathic and caring. He remarked that

it was empathy and wanting the best for the people she interacted with … she was optimistic always but she didn't want to talk very much about herself. I remember when I was in the hospital visiting her that I wanted to talk about how she was doing and she says, "Enough about me, what are you doing?" It was typical of her.[8]

Moreover, he said that

she was interested in more than just the fact that we were going to be good conductors. She was really concerned about us as individuals, she was sincerely interested in the people she was teaching. And that came through in the teaching.[9]

Elizabeth's persistence in teaching was a hallmark of her presence. Martin Haberman describes persistence in teaching as being "inextricably linked to commitment."[10] Elizabeth's persistence can be seen in her strongly held core beliefs about student learning. She believed that it was her responsibility to find ways of engaging her students in learning.[11] Moreover, Elizabeth felt a constant responsibility to make her classes interesting and engaging as well as to meet the needs of everyone in the room. This sentiment was expressed by Paula Crider, who stated: "From everything I observed about this master teacher, she was truly a caring mentor who got to know her students quite well. She seemed to possess a rare combination of demanding excellence while maintaining an encouraging presence."[12] Although Crider's interactions were limited to only a few workshops and private conducting lessons, she was able to see Elizabeth's presence from afar.

From her caring, empathy, and perhaps *motherly* nature, several informants mentioned Elizabeth's nickname beginning in the late 1950s – "ma Green." Elizabeth herself recounted the origination of this nickname, which still persists after 50 years.

> One day, a student who had just been reading a letter from his mother, asked if we could do some activity in class. I've forgotten what activity it was, by the class was not yet ready for that experience. I had to refuse his request. He wanted to argue his point, and without thinking he stuttered, "But, Ma ..." The class exploded [with laugher] and I became "Ma Green."[13]

Reynolds commented that "we called her *Ma Green* because we looked upon her as like a mother figure. We didn't call her to her face that but that's what everybody called her among each other."[14] Larry Livingston, a former student of Elizabeth's, agreed and mentioned "no one would have considered calling her Elizabeth or Ma Green. She gained our respect by the quality of her knowledge, her demeanor, her pedagogy.[15]

Drawing on the work of relational psychologists Carol Rodgers and Merriam Raider-Roth, teacher connection to students can be seen as an essential component of presence. They state that mutual empathy or "feeling seen" is the ability for a teacher to take the perspective of a student by seeing the world as the student sees it. Moreover, these psychologists suggested that mutual trust with students is central in a teacher's relational capacity to be present.[16]

Green's Relational Capacity for Cultivating Rapport and Trust

When considering the place that trust and rapport hold in human relationships, it is essential to uncover the components of a trustworthy teaching–learning relationship. Miriam Raider-Roth labels the four central features

> (1) the teacher's capacity to be connected to the student, (2) the teacher's genuine interest in nurturing the student's own ideas, (3) collaborative study on the part of the teacher and student, and (4) an environment in which trust can prevail.[17]

Informants were clear in their discussions about Elizabeth's ability to cultivate rapport and trust with her students and colleagues, and these features of trust are presented in order of their popularity among the informant interviews.

Collaborative Inquiry

One of the qualities of a trustworthy relationship is teacher–student collaborative inquiry, and this quality permeated Elizabeth's pedagogy. Whether a student was in her conducting classes, violin classes, or orchestra rehearsals, Elizabeth cultivated trust through a shared focus of studying music. Even though Dan Long was never Elizabeth's student, he was in contact with many of her students. For instance, Dan hosted over 120 student teachers at Slauson Middle School[18] (Ann Arbor, Michigan), and he remembered:

> I got this much of this information through a lot of my Student Teachers, who saw her in a different way than I did. You see, I did not see her in a classroom setting, but they did. They referred to her, when they talked about her, extremely high expectations, very high expectations. She believed that there was no substitute for quality. That you had to do it, until it was right.[19]

He also remarked that "everybody just had the highest regard for her and she was just this force."[20] Elizabeth's high expectations for her students structured the necessary scaffolding to cultivate rapport and trust with her students.

Larry Livingston, a former student of Elizabeth, confirmed these sentiments and added, "she was a wonderful musician but because of unique combination of her highly developed with a sparkling temperament that made you feel capable."[21] Livingston's memory captures this idea, where the focus of instruction shifts away from the "all-knowing" teacher to the learner who is seeking answers.

Teachers' Connectedness

Judith Palac, a former student of Elizabeth, expanded on Green's ability to cultivate rapport and trust among her students. She mentioned that

> I always felt like if she treated me as a colleague even though she had very set ideas. She didn't seem to demand that you put yourself on a pedestal. She didn't demand worship. I would say that even in those few interactions I had with her, I felt like there was a relationship of collegiality and trust.[22]

Palac was not the only former student who felt this way. Barbara Barstow, Palac's former high school orchestra teacher, remembered how

Green was always available to discuss problems in music or rehearsal strategies. Barstow explained:

> I always thought that I could call on her. And as you see she came whenever I asked her for something, she was there. I just wish there were more opportunities you know to be with her. And I think she sincerely ... she was there for her students ... any of us. That meant so much to her.[23]

One possible explanation for Green's connection to her students was that she considered her students a part of her family. Judith Palac explained that

> it was very clear to me from the way Barbara [Barstow] talked about Elizabeth that they were very close. Barbara learned about conducting from Elizabeth and Elizabeth really adopted her. I've heard of that I think that happened more in conducting class than it did in string methods.[24]

In a press release announcing her retirement from the University of Michigan, she was quoted as saying, "I worry about them. My mother used to tell me I'd be a lot better off if I didn't 'adopt' every student I had."[25] Dan Long confirmed this by noting, "you were her family. ... Every student that entered into her life, was her family. Every single one."[26]

Connectedness is a term used by a variety of disciplines, including education, music education, adolescent psychology, and nursing. Broadly, the term is defined as the psychological state in which students perceive that they and others are cared for, trusted, and respected by teachers.[27] Most of the interviewees clearly discussed Elizabeth's ability to cultivate rapport and mutual trust with her students and colleagues. The focus of their statements uncovered a term known as *connectedness*. There is a small literature base that examines the characteristics of music teachers and student–teacher relationships in music education. Music education research highlights the importance of teacher support in early music instruction.[28] This research also makes clear the positive, direct effect that teacher support has on student motivation within the context of perseverance through music instruction[29] and self-regulatory practice behaviors.[30] Moreover, some researchers report that there is a positive relationship between student-reported feelings of teacher support and their musical achievement. In a more contemporary study, Si Millican and Sommer Forrester extended this work and reported that developing knowledge of and relationships with students is a core practice needed in the music education profession.[31] The research literature on teacher–student relationships in music education parallels the empirical evidence from adolescent development, which suggests that students who report feeling cared for by teachers are more connected to their music experience. In essence,

> I think this "connection" was absolutely necessary for Ma Green. That she could reach her students on a personal level was one of her many strengths. One felt that she was genuinely interested in you as a person as well as a musician.[32]

Teachers' Genuine Interest

Another feature of trust in a teacher–student relationship is a teacher's genuine interest in student ideas.[33] Green's pedagogy reinforced her belief that students' own ideas and music connections promoted intellectual development. Dan Long described the quality of trust among Elizabeth and her students through her willingness to help them.

> You just sensed that this was the woman who would do anything to help you. She was not one to pass you off. If you took the time to want to meet her and if you took the time to want to spend some time with her, she immediately would take you under her wing. She just immediately did that. There were no reservations. No second thoughts. I remember her saying to me "Of course I will help you. That is what I am here for."[34]

One of the ways that Elizabeth established trust was through how she gave feedback to her students during classes. Given the performance outcomes of a conducting class, there were several opportunities for teacher–student instructional coaching. H. Robert Reynolds remembers a time when he was not as prepared for his conducting class coaching.

> When I was a high school student in my high school band, my band director who was very good, would ask us periodically if somebody would like to conduct through a piece of music we had been working on instead of him conducting through it. Nobody else seemed to want to do that but I did, so I kept doing it. ... When I took her [Elizabeth] first semester conducting class, I could already do a lot of it, and so when she gave us these exercises, I could just do it.

I didn't have to work at it I could just do it and other people would be just trying to figure out down, left, right, up, they were still trying to get to that point. And so one day I hadn't worked on he exercises like I usually did and I got up I thought I'd do just fine and she said, "Robert, I know what you're capable of." ... I remember where she was standing, where I was standing, it was mortifying. And I had to then from that point on, live up to what I felt that she thought I was capable of. And I didn't know how high that was but I was trying to meet that standard. ... She would in some way be like, "I know this is difficult to do but I also know you can do it." I mean she could have just said, "Don't ever stand up here prepared like that again." But she prefaced that with that one statement, "I know what you're capable of." And then that made me want to do it, not just to defend myself against her reprimands. I felt more at that point, that I disappointed her than I felt reprimanded and I knew I was wrong because I hadn't prepared. ... I didn't think I needed to because I could already do it but she clearly saw things that I wasn't doing that I should have been doing.[35]

Elizabeth's strong belief in her students' aptitude is a consistent theme with the informants and their memories. Their memories suggest that in order for students to trust their teachers, teachers need to convey curiosity about their students' ideas. Dan Long remarked that

they recognized that she believed in them, she showed them, in lots of various ways, that she believed in them, they gained this respect for her. They spoke in very endearing terms, because they knew that, yes, she did have high expectations, but at the same time they knew that she really believed that they could do it. That they had the potential of doing it, whatever it was. ... Not only did it catch your attention, but you develop this respect. You had this respect, for this woman, because you knew that she wanted the very best for you. She wanted to have you succeed, in whatever our endeavors were. No question about it. no question about it.[36]

Not only did Elizabeth believe in her student's aptitude as future musicians, she was also very interested in them as individuals. H. Robert Reynolds remembered a story when Elizabeth stopped to help him while he was an undergraduate student:

a friend of mine was going home with me to Pennsylvania for Thanksgiving and these were the days when you can actually do this, you can't do it anymore but we were hitchhiking to the airport. We each had a bag and we were standing out on Washington Avenue and Elizabeth Green drove by and she wanted to know what we were doing. We said, "We're hitchhiking to the airport to go to my home for Thanksgiving." She says, "I don't have anything to do, just get in the car I'll just take you." I mean that was typical, that wasn't out of the ordinary.[37]

A Safe Environment

In addition to a teacher's genuine interest, a teacher's ability to provide a safe environment is also a central feature. Miriam Raider-Roth explains that this last feature of mutual trust in a teacher–student relationship involves creating an environment or atmosphere in which trust can exist.[38] Dr. Daniel Siegel demonstrates that students need to have a sense of being "seen, safe, and soothed in order to feel secure," and Karyn Purvis and her colleagues clarify that being safe and feeling safe are not the same thing.[39] In uncovering this idea of safety, it is essential to ask *What aspects of safety are paramount in music learning settings?* It appears that there two clear categories of safety – physical and psychological. The first category, physical safety, refers to the learning conditions that may influence the physiological needs of the student. Abraham Maslow's Hierarchy of Needs is often referred to as a framework relating to safety, with the premise that basic human needs must be fulfilled before social, esteem, and self-actualization needs are considered.[40] Physical safety in music learning settings is essential for group-based music making. For instance, instruments and human bodies must be secure and stable so as to avoid injury. While physical safety measures are an important part of all school classrooms, students *feeling* safe in the music classroom is not the same as an adult declaration that a classroom *is* safe.

The second category, psychological safety, refers to whether it is safe to engage in interpersonal risk-taking. Musicians take interpersonal risks when they engage in group-based music making. Among the informants, only a few mentioned this aspect of Elizabeth's relational capacity; however, two informants in particular reported feeling safe in her class. Robert Phillips, a former student of Elizabeth's, remembered feeling psychologically safe in her class:

Watching her teach conducting I never felt like anybody was at risk emotionally. I always felt like it was a safe place. ... She understood that none of us had any experience at this and that we were developing musicians. ... We were not completed works, if you will. I think that she took great care to have a professional class but not one that was threatening. ... As long as you were focused on trying to get better and trying to learn what she had to teach in the conducting class she was just incredibly, supportive and kind, and she just wanted you to get better. It didn't matter whether you had naturally good baton technique or whatever it might be. That wasn't the issue, it was just helping you to get better. In other words, she didn't favor in any way somebody that had more natural, I can do it right away, ability.[41]

Phillips' memory of Elizabeth's ability to curate a safe environment was discussed at length by another former student, Robert Jager. He remarked that

there was a warmth about Elizabeth Green where the music is always ... the music and the student are the most important things in this classroom ... you felt that going into the classroom that this was going to be every time. This was going to be something special, and it was.[42]

In the interviews, some informants revealed more details about Elizabeth's ability to create a safe learning environment. Robert Jager detailed his experience with Elizabeth and explained:

She always had respect for her students and I think I learned almost as much about how to teach as I did about the subject matter because I would watch her interactions with the students and just think, "Wow, I like that." Especially after I came back from [military] service, I was older and more appreciative of the education I was getting. ... I never saw her or heard her being mean to anybody. I never heard her be rude or crude or swear. It's just wasn't her. Maybe that's part of the power of her pedagogy. I mean, it's just wonderful. I had the highest regard for her, needless to say, and I'm sure that anybody in her classes feels the same way.[43]

Elizabeth demonstrated that we, as music teachers, must protect each student's access to a safe learning space because issues of safety are paramount in music learning settings.

"People Don't Care How Much You Know Until They Know How Much You Care"[44]

> Elizabeth Green was the queen there was something ... even though she was very humble and very modest, both in her lifestyle and in the way she lived and in the way she taught and the way she was ... there was something very royal about her. When you would spend some time with her, you would sense that there was something special about her. I don't know if you would say it was something of queen-liness, although, she certainly wore a crown in many people's eyes. There was something that led you to believe that there was something that was a special thing about her. There was a sense about her.[45]

Elizabeth Green expressed care for many of her students, and as showcased earlier in the chapter, a component of Elizabeth's personality was to show care for her students. Examining music teacher personality has been a pervasive focus of music education researchers for the last 50 years.[46] Following this line of inquiry, Martin Bergee investigated the relationship between music education majors' personality profiles and indicators of music teaching success. Using the Missouri Pre-Professional Teacher Interview (MPTI), Bergee found that preservice music teachers have malleable personalities. Music teacher educators "may identify relative [personality] deficiencies and develop methods of addressing these deficiencies, teaching organizational strategies, time management, etc."[47] Almost a decade later, David Teachout called into question the inconsistency in research investigating the link between personality traits and development of teaching effectiveness. Using Holland's (1992) vocational theory, Teachout confirmed Bergee's finding of personality malleability or development over time; however, Teachout suggested that "accurately assessing the interaction between personality and music teaching effectiveness may not occur until one is stabilized in the role of 'music teacher.'"[48] It is clear there is more for researchers to investigate and uncover about music teacher personality. Chronicling Elizabeth's personality may be a unique contribution to this field of study, and the forthcoming memories detailing parts of her personality may hold true for other extraordinary music teachers.

Elizabeth was known as an authentic person. For the purposes of this chapter, authenticity is defined as a "self-conscious appropriate of the conditions of one's own existence and identity."[49] Simply put, this is the extent to which Elizabeth was true to her own character and beliefs despite the popularity of her opinion. Robert Jager recalls the honesty in her teaching and remarked:

> I think my feeling is that she was honest in her teaching. … There was never a moment that you got the feeling that she didn't know what they were talking about. … There was never any time when she belittled anyone that I knew except the one time in the Bernstein piece but she didn't even belittle him. She belittled Bernstein more than the student. … There's always, "I'm here for you. Let's make music together." That was conveyed without it being said. You just felt like this is the one figure in the school of music that you can go to about a musical problem or even a life problem. Somehow, they were related in the way she approached them.[50]

Barbara Barstow confirmed Elizabeth's honesty in her teaching by recalling an interaction close to her death.

> Oh yes, I saw Elizabeth right before she died. She was still so sharp and so she's so organized. She gave very good comments and she doesn't hold back. … Elizabeth could spot talent very easily. she never talked badly of people … she would criticize conductors that she would respect. Oh, my goodness, she would say things like "They're all over the place. There's no language." I thought of all that because she thought Seiji Osawa really had great technique and she was really insistent on that, which was interesting to me. She thought a lot of him. I remember her being pretty critical of most conductors. So, you have to be clear. … It really makes a difference. You can hear it in the orchestras.

Elizabeth was not just honest in her teaching; she was also known for her honesty in music department meetings. Larry Hurst recalled how Elizabeth taught for two departments at the University of Michigan – the String Department and Music Education Department. During the period when Larry was the String Department Chair, he mentioned that Elizabeth knew how to navigate the micropolitics of the School of Music.

> I think Elizabeth had a really good sense of how to work in that environment. Now she probably did have, I think, had a lot of knock down and drag outs with the music education department because that's about coursework that she was involved with. You know I'm sure they wanted to cut this [course] … add [that course]

that at certain points. And she probably has to defend herself with that sort of thing. ... In a string department, she just was used as kind of an advisor. We would ask her certain things about coursework and how that sort of thing has an effect at the students.[51]

Authenticity in teaching and interactions was essential for Elizabeth, and it is this honesty that is a legacy of hers, resonating throughout the music education profession.

Together with honesty, Elizabeth lived a modest lifestyle, maintaining boundaries about her privacy. Dan Long mentioned her honesty and modesty at the beginning of this section of the chapter, while Barbara Barstow remembered how music of a private person she was.

I never talked to her about my personal life, although she loved my husband. She wasn't that kind of teacher. She was more motherly. ... she was still the same person I knew since 1965. She looked exactly the same – she never changed.[52]

Larry Livingston confirmed her modesty and recalled her approach to her appearance as being a "very plain way of selecting her clothes and her hair, very perfectly appropriate and modest."[53] Alongside modesty was Elizabeth's tendency to be reserved in her personal interactions; however, she was still warm towards the people she would meet. Dan Long remembered that

she was not a person who was, out there all the time. I mean, that was just not her personality. I guess, you might describe her as being a bit reserved, at first, but not to any significant degree. She was always very welcoming.[54]

Delivering the Message Is Just as Important as the Message Itself

One of Elizabeth's gifts related to relational capacity was her ability to deliver a message to a recipient with sensitivity while also being direct. Specifically, Elizabeth knew how to talk to individuals and deliver the content or "message" so that it was meaningful and impactful to the student. This gift could not have been possible without a strong relationship, and as Barbara Barstow succinctly noted, "she was always kind ... she was always business."[55]

The interviewees' memories of Elizabeth vary in scope and depth as well as their interactions with her. Of all the interviewees, Dan Long had unique, prolonged engagement with Elizabeth and knew her in a different way than Barbara or H. Robert Reynolds. Elizabeth's relationship with Dan transformed over the years from mentor to friend. Dan was around her for extended periods of time toward the end of her life, and in almost a glimpse of terminal lucidity, Elizabeth knew that her legacy would not be kept secret.

> The relationship changed over a period of years to one where, it was still a mentorship business but, it was also a friend. She was a friend. And, I was so fortunate that we lived here in town, so, we would have her come over and have lunch with us. We would just, you know, do things socially. We would include her in Thanksgivings or Christmases or family gatherings ... it was clear that we had had a lot of conversations. Up to and even prior to that and she had never told me anything like that before. She would just give answers and that was it. But, finally at this point, after some time ... and, maybe it was when she was maybe in her late seventies, early eighties, age-wise ... that, she was beginning to think, "You know, my time on this earth is getting on the other side of the timeline, instead of at the beginning, it is now towards the end. And, I want to make sure that it is not kept a secret."[56]

H. Robert Reynolds, like Dan Long, had a unique relationship with Elizabeth Green. Elizabeth's relationship with Robert transformed over the years from mentor to friend. Robert's friendship was not entirely social. He clarified:

> Friendship, yes, but it wasn't a friend of equals. I still treated her like she deserved to be treated. I never called her Elizabeth, it was always Miss Green and I would never call her "Ma Green." She knew that people called her that. But no one ever called her that to her face. It was just too much respect and admiration for her. ... I mean you wouldn't dream of calling her anything else. Maybe Professor Green, but mostly it was Miss Green.

Moreover, Robert mentioned that

> we didn't hang out socially. We didn't go to parties together or meet for lunch. We never did anything like that. There was always a distance between us and I put the distance there. I didn't want to presume to have the association more than I knew that it was. ... I mean it morphed into a little bit more than that. Once I came on

the faculty [University of Michigan] and she was retired, then there was never any thinking she was teaching me. She was never saying, "You should do this, try this." That was gone and now there were just discussions about music and about how you taught conducting and about what's going on in the profession and things like that.

Delivering the message was important for Elizabeth, and she had to learn this skill throughout her life. As mentioned in Chapter 1, Elizabeth's first semester of teaching was not successful with regard to her relational capacity. She mentioned in an October 31, 1928, letter to her parents that she struggled with her use of humor in the junior high orchestra class. She wrote:

> Well, I got them all to laugh at themselves, and that's the first step in correcting a mistake publicly. Then I jumped on them individually at this Junior [High] Orchestra Rehearsal. We were having a great time, and even the impossible ones were getting long bows and nice wrists ... then I saw it and poor Sydney didn't have his bow on the edge at the frog. I reached over and turned it, saying, "Just a little more on the edge like this, Sydney." Well, I didn't think anything of that. I was calling everyone down. When we started the next piece, I looked at Sydney and the child was almost crying. He was just righting to keep back the tears ... it made me feel terrible to think I had hurt anyone so – especially, Sydney.[57]

The letter goes on to describe how she corrected her error; however, she was fallible. One of the reasons that this example was referenced is because of her resilience. Master teachers recognize and own up to their mistakes instead of denying them and not changing.[58] Although Elizabeth's errors in judgment were few during her career, there is evidence throughout her correspondence with her parents that when she made a lapse in judgment, she would correct herself so as to not break trust with the student.

Around the same time period, and while observing Elizabeth teach at the University of Michigan, Larry Hurst remembered that Elizabeth was

> not only was she a very skilled musician, teacher, diagnostician and technician, but her ability to get to get to the core of what and how you needed to hear something. And she had a very unique way of doing that and she knew how to approach you. ... She had a way of breaking down instruction to its simplest form that served up but it wasn't dumbed down.[59]

Elizabeth was just as adept in the junior high school classes as with her university students. Dan Long described a time when he had Elizabeth present a clinic to his students at Slauson Junior High School (Elizabeth's former orchestra program). He connected how Elizabeth's pedagogy included not just instrument-specific pedagogy, but also knowing how the students needed to hear the message.

> Her teaching was like a rubber band. You stretch it. And you work hard and then there is the time where you have to go – "Whew!" And let it go back to its natural shape and have that light moment and then stretch it again and then let it come back. Because, if you stretch a rubber band and continually hold it there, it will not return to its original shape if you keep holding it there. It loses its original shape. Well, the same with her teaching. She would really focus and work hard and stretch, stretch, stretch, work, work, work, high expectations – and then, "Whew – alright, let's go back and do it again." She was a master at that. So, whenever you have these sessions or whenever you would see her working with an orchestra. Yeah, she would do that. That would be one of the things she would do. You know, just let it return to its shape. Now, let's go back and work again.[60]

Figure 4.1 Michael Avsharian (left), Elizabeth Green (center), Charles Avsharian (right), circa 1993.

Source: Elizabeth Green Papers (SC-32), Buswell Library Special Collections, Wheaton, Illinois.

"An experience is always what it is because of a transaction taking place between an individual and what, at the time, constitutes his (*sic*) environment."[61] It may be that there are universal pedagogical qualities of exceptional teachers; however, there is little research about how music teachers develop relationships with students or how music teacher education prepares future and in-service teachers to do this work. On the other hand, and as stated by Dewey, it stands to reason that the unique combination of the pedagogical characteristics and relational capacities that each teacher possesses balances a memorable experience.

Notes

1 Arvil S. Barr, "The Measurement and Prediction of Teaching Efficiency: A Summary of Investigations," *Journal of Experimental Education* 16, no. 4 (1948): 203–283.
2 Jennifer A. Robinson, "A Study of Inspiring Australian Music Teachers," master's thesis, University of Sydney, Sydney Australia, 2015. Retrieved from https://hdl.handle.net/2123/14158.
3 Carol R. Rodgers and Miriam B. Raider-Roth, "Presence in Teaching," *Teachers and Teaching: Theory and Practice* 12, no. 3 (2006): 265.
4 Shannan L. Hibbard, "Music Teacher Presence: Toward a Relational Understanding," Ph.D. diss., University of Michigan, Ann Arbor, ProQuest Dissertations and Theses Global (UMI No. 10760119): 7.
5 Long interview, September 28, 2017.
6 Long interview, October 3, 2017.
7 Long interview, September 28, 2017.
8 Reynolds interview, October 9, 2017.
9 Reynolds interview, January 22, 1986, quoted in Deborah Annette Smith, "Elizabeth A. H. Green: A Biography," Ph.D. diss., University of Michigan, Ann Arbor, 1986, ProQuest Dissertations and Theses Global (UMI No. 8621380), 108.
10 Martin Haberman, *Star Teachers: The Ideology and Best Practice of Effective Teachers of Diverse Children and Youth in Poverty* (Haberman Educational Foundation, 2005).
11 Folder 31, Correspondence 1964, Bulletins, Box 2, Folder 31. Elizabeth Green Papers, SC-032. Buswell Library Special Collections.
12 Crider interview, January 8, 2018.
13 Green interview, March 18, 1985, quoted in Deborah Annette Smith, "Elizabeth A. H. Green: A Biography," Ph.D. diss., University of Michigan, Ann Arbor, 1986, ProQuest Dissertations and Theses Global (UMI No. 8621380), 108.
14 Reynolds interview, October 9, 2017.
15 Livingston interview, October 12, 2020.
16 Rodgers and Raider-Roth, 267.

17 Miriam Raider-Roth. *Trusting What You Know: The High Stakes of Classroom Relationships* (San Francisco: John Wiley & Sons, Inc., 2005), 29–30.

18 Jared R. Rawlings, "Don't Keep It a Secret": E. Daniel Long and His Career in Music Education," *Journal of Historical Research in Music Education* 42, no. 2 (2021): 159–179.

19 Long interview, September 28, 2017.

20 Ibid.

21 Livingston interview, October 12, 2020.

22 Palac interview, August 4, 2018.

23 Barstow interview, May 21, 2018.

24 Palac interview, August 4, 2018.

25 Report of Faculty Retirement, July 1974, News and Information Services, Box 5, Folder 8, University of Michigan Archives, Ann Arbor.

26 Long interview, September 28, 2017.

27 Clea McNeely, Janis Whitlock, and Heather Libbey, "School Connectedness and Adolescent Well-Being," in *Handbook of School–Family Partnerships*, eds. S. L. Christenson and A. L. Reschly (New York: Routledge, 2010), 266–386.

28 Jane W. Davidson, Derek G. Moore, John A. Sloboda, and Michael J. A. Howe, "Characteristics of Music Teachers and the Progress of Young Instrumentalists," *Journal of Research in Music Education* 46, no. 1 (1998): 141–160; Donald M. Taylor, "Support Structures Contributing to Instrument Choice and Achievement Among Texas All-State Male Flutists," *Bulletin of the Council for Research in Music Education* (2009): 45–60.

29 Stephanie E. Pitts, Jane W. Davidson, and Gary E. McPherson, "Models of Success and Failure in Instrumental Learning: Case Studies of Young Players in the First 20 Months of Learning," *Bulletin of the Council for Research in Music Education* (2000): 51–69; Anne Power, "What Motivates and Engages Boys in Music Education?" *Bulletin of the Council for Research in Music Education* (2008): 85–102.

30 Davidson et al., 1998.

31 Si J. Millican and Sommer H. Forrester, "Core Practices in Music Teaching: A Delphi Expert Panel Survey," *Journal of Music Teacher Education* 27, no. 3 (2018): 51–64; Si J. Millican and Sommer H. Forrester, "Music Teacher Rankings of Selected Core Teaching Practices," *Journal of Music Teacher Education* 29, no. 1 (2019): 86–99.

32 Crider interview, January 8, 2018.

33 Raider-Roth, 31.

34 Long interview, September 28, 2017.

35 Reynolds interview, October 9, 2017.

36 Long interview, October 3, 2017.

37 Reynolds interview, October 9, 2017.

38 Raider-Roth, 33.

39 Daniel J. Siegel, *Brainstorm: The Power and Purpose of the Teenage Brain* (New York: Penguin, 2015), 145; Karyn B. Purvis, David R. Cross, and

Wendy L. Sunshine, "Disarming the Fear Response with Felt Safety," in *The Connected Child* (New York: McGraw-Hill, 2007), 47–72.

40 Abraham H. Maslow, "A Theory of Human Motivation," *Psychological Review* 50, (1943): 370–396.

41 Phillips interview, March 7, 2018.

42 Jager interview, October 4, 2018.

43 Ibid.

44 Theodore Roosevelt, n.d.

45 Long interview, September 27, 2017.

46 Lionel Kaplan, "The Relationship Between Certain Personality Characteristics and Achievement in Instrumental Music," Ph.D. diss., New York University, New York, 1961, ProQuest Dissertations and Theses Global (UMI No. 6102553); Martin J. Bergee, "The Relationship Between Music Education Majors' Personality Profiles, Other Education Majors' Profiles, and Selected Indicators of Music Teaching Success," *Bulletin of the Council for Research in Music Education* (1992): 5–15; David J. Teachout, "The Relationship Between Personality and the Teaching Effectiveness of Music Student Teachers," *Psychology of Music* 29, no. 2 (2001): 179–192; Christin Reardon MacLellan, "Differences in Myers-Briggs Personality Types Among High School Band, Orchestra, and Choir Members," *Journal of Research in Music Education* 59, no. 1 (2011): 85–100.

47 Bergee, 13.

48 Teachout, 190.

49 Michael E. Zimmerman, *Eclipse of the Self: The Development of Heidegger's Concept of Authenticity* (Ohio, 1986); Michael E. Zimmerman, *Heidegger, Authenticity, and Modernity: Essays in Honor of Hubert L. Dreyfus* (MIT, 2000).

50 Jager interview, October 4, 2018.

51 Hurst interview, May 20, 2018.

52 Barstow interview, May 21, 2018.

53 Livingston interview, October 12, 2020.

54 Long interview, September 28, 2017.

55 Barstow interview, May 21, 2018.

56 Long interview, September 28, 2017.

57 Folder 2, Correspondence 1929, Bulletins, Box 2, Folder 2. Elizabeth Green Papers, SC-032. Buswell Library Special Collections.

58 Haberman, 187.

59 Hurst interview, May 20, 2018.

60 Long interview, September 28, 2017.

61 John Dewey, *Experience and Education* (New York: Collier Books, 1938), 41.

5 Always Teaching

A teacher affects eternity; he can never tell where his influence stops.
– Henry Adams, *The Education of Henry Adams* (c. 1907)

"Don't Keep It a Secret"

Robert Jager, a former student, mentioned: "I have the feeling that she always felt that if you don't relay the message ... you let the information die with you."[1] In the spirit of this section of the chapter, "don't keep it a secret" was Elizabeth's advice to Dan Long, first discussed in Chapter 4; she was also quoted saying "my goal, all along, has been to get to the finest teachers available and then bring their professional ways of doing things into the instructional field in the schools as rapidly as possible."[2] Throughout Elizabeth's career as a music educator and music teacher educator, she was committed to sharing wisdom and knowledge with as many people as she could, never keeping what she had learned "a secret." According to Judith Palac, Elizabeth "was such a believer in public school music and that's how she started."[3] Similarly, Barbara Barstow shared that

> whatever age it is that you're conducting, you really you must give them your all and give them your best. I know I was so successful because of her [Elizabeth] and that instilling in me that "you're a music educator but that's what you are on the podium. It doesn't matter who you are conducting." I learned so much from her.[4]

Her commitment to this maxim and to public school music was displayed through dozens of workshops, clinics, guest conducting engagements, publications, and translations, which mainstreamed string and conducting pedagogy for the field of music education.

DOI: 10.4324/9781003152415-5

Planting Seeds of Curiosity

One prominent feature of Elizabeth's commitment to disseminating knowledge was how she would *plant seeds* of curiosity with her students and insist on maintaining high intellectual and musical standards. Dan Long, a former colleague and friend, mentioned,

> she was a very good seed planter. She would ask the questions, in such a way, that you knew what she was getting at. Then, she would give you a chance to answer it, a second time around, if necessary."[5]

In the interviews with Elizabeth's former students, many of them discussed the way she demonstrated *how* to be curious. H. Robert Reynolds mentioned that Elizabeth

> taught you how to be. I mean she didn't have to say, "You need to be dedicated." You'd just observe that of her and try to live up to that. In addition to teaching conducting technique, she taught life by example.[6]

Teaching by example explains a prominent characteristic of Elizabeth – her integrity. According to H. Robert Reynolds, Elizabeth also believed that "telling isn't teaching." He stated that

> it's [pedagogy] more than modeling ... it's the fact that you are doing what you're teaching and so the teaching isn't only a theoretical researched scholarly endeavor ... she did what she was teaching other people to do. She would always say "Telling isn't teaching."[7]

Elizabeth was often seen treating others better than she treated herself. Her commitment to serving others may be connected to her strongly held core religious beliefs, and this association is a plausible explanation for her robust integrity. Larry Hurst, a former student and colleague, mentioned that "she epitomized the dedication and knowledgeable teacher; one that could inspire as well as educate."[8]

Wisdom and Knowledge

As a voracious reader and consumer of information, Elizabeth Green acquired much wisdom and knowledge over the course of her life. During her teaching at the University of Michigan, she would find many reasons to incorporate her wisdom into her classes. Whether her wisdom was captured in an anecdote or a class exercise, Elizabeth's students knew that she was intentional and malleable when it came to her teaching. Larry Livingston mentioned that

> she treated us with great respect and admiration and with a smile. I think, in the back of her head, she knew not all of these people are going to get all of this right away, but I'm in it for the long haul.[9]

Elizabeth knew from her years of teaching public school that not all students learn at the same pace and that some students need differentiated instruction.

Elizabeth had a direct way of sharing her knowledge at the University of Michigan, and occasionally this affected her popularity among the students. While Elizabeth's relational capacity was highly developed, there were some moments in her teaching when her work was "no nonsense." Larry Hurst, a former student and then-colleague at Michigan, recalled Elizabeth's "no nonsense – get it done in short order"[10] style of teaching. He went on to say that "she got results immediately and the students who could hear the difference, knew it worked. ... Because she has such an appreciation for the geniuses of our business ... being popular was not her thing."[11] Elizabeth's direct manner of teaching inspired Larry's teaching at the university level, a style he emulated at the University of Michigan and University of Indiana-Bloomington.

Although most students revered Elizabeth Green, not all students respected her pedagogy or approach to the university classroom. Whether it was immaturity or overt disrespect motivating disruptive behavior in class, Elizabeth had it under control. Barbara Barstow, a former student and friend, reported that

> some of the kids did not respect her. They just thought it was a joke – it really was awful. I bet they are kicking themselves now and Elizabeth knew they would. They were making fun of her. ... The boys especially. You know they didn't take her seriously and I was thinking "Oh God, this woman is a genius. She's given the tools of her lifetime here" and the boys were sloughing off – not showing up. It was really disgusting. Some of those boys probably are mad at themselves now or not paying attention and getting the most out of it.[12]

Despite some of the students not respecting Elizabeth's wisdom and knowledge, there were students that were impacted by her pedagogy, and some of their recollections appear toward the end of this chapter.

Passing the Baton

Elizabeth Green's approach to wisdom and knowledge was to pass as much of this information on as often as possible, or *passing the baton*, so to speak. The majority of the collective memories of Elizabeth's philosophy center on her retirement; however, there is much evidence to demonstrate that she was passing the baton throughout her entire career as a music educator and music teacher educator. Dan Long, a former colleague and friend, explained about her philosophy of passing information to others. He remembers Elizabeth saying to him, "I've had a lot of wonderful people enter into my life when I was learning. Mr. Malko and all the rest of these people. My own father ..."[13] All of her teachers that have been a part of her life had passed on to her something that they got from somebody else. Elizabeth passed knowledge on to other people who would then pass it on to somebody else. Dan Long clarified that "when she says, 'Don't keep it a secret ...' ... what she is really saying is, pass it on."[14] He remembered another instance of hearing this advice during a music lesson that he was having with Elizabeth. Dan remarked:

> She would say in our lessons "Well, let's get down to business." So, I opened up my score or whatever it was and we talked about it. And, unlike most other times, when she always had some response ... unlike those other times, she didn't say anything ... she just sat there. And, a bit of time went by, a few seconds – maybe ten seconds. And then she said to me, "Dan, I've got a couple of ideas that I will share with you, but first, you must make me a promise." I looked at her, and I said, "Well, of course, Ms. Green. What would you like me to promise?" As an aside, I could not imagine anything that she would ask me that I would not promise. I mean, it was this woman that I expected, this mentor of mine and I thought, of course I'll promise. And, she looked at me with a bit of a smile and said, "You must promise me that what I tell you, you will not keep it a secret."

During the final years of Elizabeth's life, she was intentionally asking her colleagues and friends to keep passing on information and to never hold on to it.

Dan Long also remembered a time when he hosted a pizza party for Elizabeth and some mutual friends, including William Revelli (1902–1994), Professor Emeritus and Director of Bands, University of Michigan. Dan remarked:

It was now toward the end of her life, within the last few years. It was, at the same time, Dr. Revelli, getting to the end of his life, and he was now at home. I said to Dr. Revelli, "Dr. Revelli, is there anything that I can do for you?" Because he couldn't get out, he was now at home. He said, "Yes. There's something you can do for me. They won't let me eat pizza and I would like to have some pizza." So, I went home, and I was telling my wife about that, and she said, "You know, let's see if we can somehow get him to our house and we'll have pizza here." Then she said to me, "I know what ... let's invite Elizabeth Green to come to. Let's invite Elizabeth to come." Elizabeth was still driving at the time. But, he [Dr. Revelli], of course, he was not. So, Elizabeth drove over to our house and after dinner those two started talking, and Elizabeth said, "You know, all these years, that we were colleagues, at the university, at the same time. We just never had the time to sit down and do something like this ... we just never had or took the time to sit down and socialize." ... The two of them we're just having this wonderful exchange, back and forth, and she's giving him this conducting lesson. ... She said to him, "We've got to get together again, to continue this conversation. We've got to get together, because, this is just the beginning." ... He died, within two months of that pizza party. But that was a special, special moment. She talked about that, later on, about how wonderful it was to get together and have those moments together with Bill ...[15]

Always Learning

Another prominent feature of Elizabeth's philosophy and commitment to the music education profession was her love of and her passion for learning. From early in her career as a music educator, Elizabeth was curious. Her curiosity manifested in seeking out answers to questions about string pedagogy and how to be a great conductor. Dan Long mentioned that, for her, "there's no problem that is not solvable. ... Time was not important to her. What was important to her, was getting it done right."[16] Moreover, Elizabeth's example of having a love of and passion for learning influenced other string pedagogues in the field of music education. Judith Palac, a former student, remarked:

I remember thinking that I wanted to pattern my career after Ms. Green. I wasn't ever going to get my doctorate. I was going to go have this great teaching experience and then get a university job just like she did, somewhere I could teach pedagogy and be the string teacher. I wound up going back to school, of course, but she really was an inspiration to me. Now, in retirement, I still think of her. ... She was such a great example of somebody who never quit learning.[17]

Elizabeth was a dedicated learner, and in Chapter 2, I discussed the details relating to her continued study with conducting pedagogue Nicoli Malko and internationally renowned violinist Ivan Galamian. Going forward, I showcase some of the additional projects that Elizabeth engaged with during her life, post-retirement.

The Human Brain

One of Elizabeth's fascinations and curiosities was with the human brain. Throughout the late 1970s and 1980s, there are many references to her studying the brain and writings on brain function and cognition; she also completed a keynote address on the brain at the University of Connecticut in 1978. Dan Long remembered this conversation when he was talking with Elizabeth.

one day, we were having a conversation. And, I said: "Well, tell me Ms. Green, what kinds of things are going through your mind right now?" She said, "Well, let me tell you something. There was a point where I thought my brain wasn't working as well as I thought it should. So, I called up the local geriatric center, here in town, and said, 'Do you have any classes or sessions on the brain and maintaining a healthy brain?'" The receptionist said "Oh, yea, we've got this great class. C'mon down. It meets every evening at 4 o'clock." And, she signed up for the class. So, she went to her very first class and she said, "There were about twelve of them sitting around the room. And, the leader or teacher of the class said, 'The first activity that we are going to do is, we are going to go around and learn people's names. And, you need to somehow tell the rest of the people in the room what would be a good way to try to remember your name. ... How would you use some crutch, some way of remembering that.'" She said, "I was very happy I was not first." So, it gave her some time to think about what she was going to say when it came her time. Well, she soon discovered, no more than three or four people into it, that she was already going to forget somebody's name. You know, "My name is so and so ..." And she is going, "Oh my gosh ..." Because, she knew what the test was going to be. ... "Now, how many names can you remember?"

So, she said, "I decided I needed to somehow help myself out, give myself a little assistant." Because, they were very close to each other, she did not want people to see what she was writing down on her piece of paper. So, she said, "I know what I am going to do." So, she started writing these descriptions in her own mind – "This woman as red hair ..." Then, she would write down what her name was. But, she did not want people to see how she was writing this down. So, what was she doing? She was writing all of this in Russian ... so that, people would not know what she was doing. So, she was writing all of these clues in Russian. And she said, "Oh, I'm ready." And, people would look and say, "This lady is writing something weird over here" So, finally, it comes around to her. And she said, "My name is Elizabeth Green. I am the queen of Spring." Do you see how she got that? Queen – Elizabeth, Green – Spring. The queen of Spring. And so, the first thing that comes to my mind, of course, when someone says, "What comes to mind when you hear the name Elizabeth Green?" I immediately say, "The queen of Spring." And, she had that as a way of telling others. She told me that story and I said, "Ms. Green, you did not need to go to another class when you are sitting there writing notes to yourself in Russian. There is nothing wrong with your brain."[18]

Elizabeth's self-diagnosis of her brain (mal)function was clearly a reflection of her hypersensitivity to the world around her. Her keen analytic, diagnostic, and systematic process for observation and awareness helped her throughout her life to become self-actualized.

Visual Art

During retirement, Elizabeth wanted to dedicate time to becoming a visual artist. She enrolled in an undergraduate BFA program in visual art at Eastern Michigan University, during which time she took limited speaking or performing engagements so as to focus on becoming a visual artist. Dan Long remembered the context of Elizabeth starting this third degree.

Stop and think when this woman retired, at age 69, because it was mandatory retirement. You had to retire if you were a public employee for the State of Michigan. As a University of Michigan employee, you had to retire at 69. Now, that law has changed because they took that to the State Supreme Court, and said,

"This is age discrimination. You can't make somebody retire, just because they're 69 years old." But back in those days, she had to. What did she do, when she retired? She turned around and became a student. She became an undergraduate and went to Eastern Michigan University, signed up as an art major. She was this amazing woman. So, she said, "All right, so now I'm retired. They're making me retire, so what do I do?" She did not take any workshops. She did not take any engagements, to do anything. She just devoted the next four years of her life, going to school. What does that say about a person? Someone who has that focus in their life?[19]

Indeed, Dan poses an interesting question about what this says about Elizabeth Green. From the previous chapters and recollections from her former students, colleagues, and friends, it seems like Elizabeth's intellectual curiosity was a significant force in how she chose to live her life after her parents passed away in 1962 and 1963. She clearly had high expectations for herself and what she was supposed to accomplish during her life.

One of the secondary ideas that emerged from the interviews was the notion that Elizabeth had highly developed expectations for not only her life and career, but for others, too. Her high expectations also extended to her students. Dan Long remarked: "She not only held you to a high expectation, she held herself to the same degree. In other words, she practiced what she preached ... she preached what she practiced."[20] Elizabeth's high expectations of her students manifested in demanding their best performance on a specific task at hand. Paula Crider remembers Elizabeth's demanding nature; however, it was never punitive. Paula mentioned that "she was kind, but demanding. She had that rare ability to make students work hard so as to never disappoint."[21]

Though Elizabeth seemed to have highly developed expectations, there was another side to these expectations, or being a motivator, encouraging a demanding lifestyle. In the interviews with her former students, there were only a few instances in their memories of Elizabeth Green that could be labeled humility, vulnerability, or even self-doubt. Larry Hurst, a former student and colleague of Elizabeth, remarked that

she was focused and serious about the business of teaching just as much as anybody that has to be really good all the time. Now that I think of it, she was never. ... I never saw her have a bad day and I'm sure she did.[22]

The idea of Elizabeth having a bad day was not often reported or seen within her paper collections. During the interviews, there were few examples of Elizabeth's fallibility. Considering this moment in history, it is not unusual that no mentions of a lack of open vulnerability appeared within her paper collections. Appearing strong was probably a needed characteristic of female leaders, while showing feelings or downfalls was not an acceptable social norm.[23] Barbara Barstow, a former student, mentioned Elizabeth's vulnerability when recalling a time she asked Elizabeth to conduct an honor orchestra event in Dundee, Illinois.

> Well, I asked EG to come and conduct. And I can remember this so well she did the arrangement of Tchaikovsky's Romeo and Juliet that was one of the pieces. It was so interesting. first class musician-conductor ... she kept asking: "Do you think I'm doing okay?" I'm sitting and watching my idol work with these kids because I've never seen her work with children. So, to see her with young kids and she was worried about that because was older. Well maybe 60s. she related great to them and to watch her conducting. ... It was it was a superb performance. I just remember her being so humble. I said to her "Miss Green, how could you ever question yourself?" Elizabeth said "you never stop learning and you never stop questioning."[24]

Green's Impact on Her Students' Lives and Music Education

Undeniably, Elizabeth Green influenced the pedagogy of multiple generations of music educators, and her impact on the music education profession is immeasurable. Robert Phillips, a former student of Elizabeth's, remarked,

> I guess the only thing I would say is I think she had an incredible, lasting impact on at least two generations, if not three generations, of people, and especially teachers in Michigan. Anybody that had Ma Green, it was one of your most important experiences as a university student. She was just an amazing mind and an amazing intellect. She had an incredible way of breaking things down, analyzing it, but also inspiring you to want to be better, to be the best player, best conductor, best whatever. I think it was because she was just so committed to excellence. That was just her standard that if you're going to do something, you're going to be great at it. You're going to do it to the best of your ability. I think that attitude came across every day. Every minute you spent with her was exactly that.

You just really wanted to aspire to be much better than you were, that's what she did for me.[25]

In this statement from a public school string music educator in Michigan, Robert captured the essence of Elizabeth's impact on his life and career as a music educator, as well as the breadth of her influence. He went on to make clear that

I'm almost 65 years old and I was in her last class, 1974 probably, and I've been talking about her conducting and her as a person my whole life. I can't believe how I can still stand up in front of a crowd of teachers, nobody was born then, and how many of them know about her. It's astounding and it's just amazing to me. I think she's had an enormous impact because I think one of the things that she did that might be unique is I think she was equally passionate about teaching conductors no matter what their discipline was.

I think she's one of the people that helped band directors think about conducting with artistry. ... I think she really brought artistry to the study of conducting and it's because she was a great violinist and a great musician. A lot of people don't know that she never had an education class in her life. She never studied education. She was just a performance major and a great player who worked it backwards from that. But she was a process person so her ability to analyze and dissect was unparalleled. I think what she did with conducting pedagogy in terms of dissecting it and thinking about it, and of course her work with Malko, I think she really helped do that for conducting nationally. She really helped people to understand the pedagogical .... and how to communicate artistry through conducting ... she really emphasized that you should be able to see the music in the stick motions, and in the arm motion, everything, including the facial expressions. In other words, if you're not conducting the music then what are you doing? You're just beating time. That was one of her big things.[26]

In his memories of Elizabeth, Robert was able to attribute his own practice as a string music teacher to what she taught him. He remarked:

She just made a tremendous difference in my ability to communicate clearly with an orchestra. Here's how it affected my teaching: I saw two very different roles. There are times when I'm a string teacher, and when I'm doing that I've got a violin in my hand and I'm walking around the room and I'm teaching. If I'm conducting, I'm conducting. What she taught me to do is don't stand on the podium, to me, I think of the podium as a sacred ground – don't stand on the podium unless you're going to do something communicative with your hands. If you're not, then don't wave them. I spent a lot of my teaching career not waving my hands, unless the students were ready for it and unless I was ready to communicate something with them.[27]

Expanding Elizabeth's reach from beyond the State of Michigan, former student Larry Livingston described her impact on how music teacher educators structure curriculum for preservice music teachers.

When I look back on Elizabeth's life, I more highly valued the privilege of being her student. I valued them but in subsequent years, the index of admiration and appreciation has rocketed up virtually every year. Because the stuff that she taught us, I've been able to use and pass on. ... She made the conducting technique and the protocols of conducting a worthy component in the education of the future high school and public school teachers. And that was her long history, she was a bright light in Music Education Department at Michigan when I was there.[28]

Larry's memory of Elizabeth's legacy in music education is very powerful considering the prominence of his academic positions as faculty and administrator leading conservatories of music within the United States. Over the course of his career, Larry has seen hundreds of talented musicians and teachers in many of the centering conservatories; his words about Elizabeth speak to the influence and impact of her legacy.

H. Robert Reynolds had strong feelings about Elizabeth Green's impact on his life as well as the music education profession, at large. He remarked that Elizabeth was the best teacher he ever had, and this was because of how she knew pedagogy and also had incredible awareness and relational capacity.

Logically she gave me the foundation of conducting. But then through example she taught me how to teach. It wasn't like, "Okay these are the techniques of teaching." She didn't do that but through the way she taught and the way she treated people because I had a variety of teachers both here and in my past and a lot of them were very good. But none of them combined the humanness and the teaching technique and the skill and the knowledge, that whole package." ... You could ask any of those people that went to school with me, "Who's the best teacher you've ever had?" And everybody would say, "Elizabeth Green." Immediately that's what they would say. And then you'd say, "Thank you now who's the second best teacher you've ever had?" And they'd say, "Well, let me think about that. I've had a lot of great teachers but I need to think about that a little bit ... but nobody had to think about who was the best.[29]

One way of recognizing Elizabeth's impact on the field of string music education was the creation of the Elizabeth A. H. Green School Educator Award, sponsored by the American String Teachers Association. Dan Long was the first awardee of this honor, and he mentioned, in a published oral history,

I was awarded the first one [ASTA Elizabeth A. H. Green Award] and I'm proud of that. It was very special. An award that is named after someone that you had such high regard and high respect for and then to receive that in her name. It's just a wonderful thing. It's extremely special for me and so gratifying and ... I was so humbled and honored knowing that this woman represented the best of everything in music education – the best! ... Of course Elizabeth's award meant a great deal to me.[30]

Dan also shared that

she had a profound impact on me. Profound impact on me. I mean, here was this kid, from the Sand Hills of Nebraska, who knew nothing about string playing, nothing. Then, just learned from the master. ... Elizabeth Green was one of the people who was so generous, and so kind, and so caring, and all those words that come to my mind.[31]

Dan Long established a strong mentor/mentee relationship with Green over the span of almost 30 years. His conversations with Green ranged from interpretive decisions about music notation to understanding conducting movement to string pedagogy.

Overall, Elizabeth's impact on the music education profession reverberates today. Paula Crider commented:

Elizabeth Green is an icon. She influenced an entire generation of young conductors in a most positive and profound manner. I would be remiss if I did not mention the fact that she was the first female role model for many women conductors. … My lessons with Maestra Green represented a brief time in my career … but had a profound effect on my development as a musician and as a conductor.[32]

Paula also credited *The Modern Conductor* with having a lasting impact on the music education profession and explained that

her book made a profound difference in the manner in which conducting was taught. She was the first in our profession to investigate split brain theory. Her greatest impact, of course, is the

Figure 5.1 Elizabeth Green during her retirement, circa 1993.
Source: Used with permission by MLive Media Group.

fact that she positively impacted an entire generation of young conductors, who in turn, took the art of non-verbal communication to even higher levels of artistry. ... Elizabeth Green's contributions continue to be reflected in her students.[33]

Notes

1 Jager interview, October 4, 2018.
2 Elizabeth A. H. Green, quoted in Traugott Rohner, ed., "People of Note," *The Instrumentalist* 16, no. 8 (April 1962): 82.
3 Palac interview, August 4, 2018.
4 Barstow interview, May 21, 2018.
5 Long interview, September 28, 2017.
6 Reynolds interview, October 9, 2017.
7 Ibid.
8 Hurst interview, May 20, 2018.
9 Livingston interview, October 12, 2020.
10 Hurst interview, May 20, 2018.
11 Ibid.
12 Barstow interview, May 21, 2018.
13 Long interview, September 28, 2017.
14 Ibid.
15 Ibid.
16 Ibid.
17 Palac interview, August 4, 2018.
18 Long interview, September 27, 2017.
19 Ibid.
20 Ibid.
21 Crider, January 8, 2018.
22 Hurst interview, May 20, 2018.
23 Jacqueline S. Smith, Victoria L. Brescoll, and Erin L. Thomas, "Constrained by Emotion: Women, Leadership, and Expressing Emotion in the Workplace," in *Handbook on Well-Being of Working Women*, eds. Mary L. Connerley and Jiyun Wu (Springer, Dordrecht, 2016), 209–224.
24 Barstow interview, May 21, 2018.
25 Phillips interview, March 7, 2018.
26 Ibid.
27 Ibid.
28 Livingston interview, October 12, 2020.
29 Reynolds interview, October 9, 2017.
30 Rawlings, 2021, 178.
31 Long interview, September 28, 2017.
32 Crider, January 8, 2018.
33 Ibid.

Appendix A
Selected Publications

Journal Articles

Green, Elizabeth A. H., "Orchestra Courtesy." *The School Musician* (February 1933), 14–15, 40.

Green, Elizabeth A. H., "String in Solo vs. Orchestra Playing." *The School Musician* (March 1933), 18–19.

Green, Elizabeth A. H., "Do You Look the Part." *The School Musician* (April 1933), 16, 37.

Green, Elizabeth A. H., "Fiddle, Do You Really Play?" *The School Musician* (May 1933), 12, 41.

Green, Elizabeth A. H., "String Tone." *The School Musician* (September 1936), 19, 35–36.

Green, Elizabeth A. H., "Waterloo's Port of Rescue for Vanishing School Musicians." *The School Musician* (October 1936), 18, 19.

Green, Elizabeth A. H., "Miss Green Brings You a Rehearsal." *The School Musician* (January 1937) 6, no. 5, 19.

Green, Elizabeth A. H., "This Thing Called Color." *The School Musician* (March 1937), 6, no. 7, 42, 44, 46.

Green, Elizabeth A. H., "Trends in Instrumental Music Teaching." *Music Educators Journal* (September 1937), 24, no. 1, 36–39.

Green, Elizabeth A. H., "The Greatest Need?" *Music Educators Journal* (October 1938), 25, no. 2, 35, 37.

Green, Elizabeth A. H., "The School Orchestra Stakes Out Its Claim." *The School Musician* (January 1941), 13, no. 5, 10–12.

Green, Elizabeth A. H., "The School Orchestra Challenges the Band." *The School Musician* (April 1942), 13, no. 8, 6–9.

Green, Elizabeth A. H., "Strings." *The School Musician* (September 1942), 14, no. 1, 8–9.

Green, Elizabeth A. H., "The Teaching of Strings." *The Etude* (October 1943), 61, no. 10, 647–648.

Green, Elizabeth A. H., "Creating Interest in Strings." *The School Musician* (January 1945), 16, no. 5, 19, 31.

Green, Elizabeth A. H., "Developing String Players." *The School Musician* (February 1945), 16, no. 6, 8–9, 34.

Green, Elizabeth A. H., "Tots and Strings." *The Etude* (April 1945), 63, no. 4, 232.

Green, Elizabeth, A. H., "Pleasure and Profit." *Michigan Education Journal* (April 1945), 392.

Green, Elizabeth A. H., "Eyes to See." *The Etude* (May 1945), 63, no. 5, 258, 288.

Green, Elizabeth A. H., "Orchestra Bowing for High School Students." *The Etude* (June 1945), 63, no. 6, 318, 350, 360.

Green, Elizabeth A. H., "Strings: The Strength of the Orchestra." *The School Musician* (December 1945), 17, no. 4, 24–26.

Green, Elizabeth A. H., "Strings: The Strength of the Orchestra." *The School Musician* (January 1946), 17, no. 6, 28–29.

Green, Elizabeth A. H., "Strings: The Strength of the Orchestra." *The School Musician* (February 1946), 17, no. 7, 28–29.

Green, Elizabeth A. H., "Strings: The Strength of the Orchestra." *The School Musician* (March 1946), 17, no. 8, 40–41.

Green, Elizabeth A. H., "Strings: The Strength of the Orchestra." *The School Musician* (April 1946), 17, no. 9, 29, 32.

Green, Elizabeth A. H., "Strings: The Strength of the Orchestra." *The School Musician* (May 1946), 17, no. 10, 32–33.

Green, Elizabeth A. H., "Strings: The Strength of the Orchestra." *The School Musician* (June 1946), 17, no. 11, 29–31.

Green, Elizabeth A. H., "Strings: The Strength of the Orchestra." *The School Musician* (September 1946), 18, no. 2, 46–47.

Green, Elizabeth A. H., "Strings: The Strength of the Orchestra." *The School Musician* (October 1946), 18, no. 3, 25.

Green, Elizabeth A. H., "Strings: The Strength of the Orchestra." *The School Musician* (November 1946), 18, no. 4, 34–35.

Green, Elizabeth A. H., "Strings: The Strength of the Orchestra." *The School Musician* (December 1946), 18, no. 5, 32–33.

Green, Elizabeth A. H., "Strings: The Strength of the Orchestra." *The School Musician* (January 1947), 18, no. 6, 36–37.

Green, Elizabeth A. H., "Strings: The Strength of the Orchestra." *The School Musician* (February 1947), 18, no. 7, 28–29.

Green, Elizabeth A. H., "Strings: The Strength of the Orchestra." *The School Musician* (March 1947), 18, no. 8, 32–33.

Green, Elizabeth A. H., "Strings: The Strength of the Orchestra." *The School Musician* (April 1947), 18, no. 9, 32–33.

Green, Elizabeth A. H., "Michigan Makes Music With Strings." *The Instrumentalist* (March–April 1947), 1, no. 8, 4.

Green, Elizabeth A. H., "Strings: The Strength of the Orchestra." *The School Musician* (May 1947), 65, no. 5, 256, 286, 293.

Green, Elizabeth A. H., "How Music Helps With Other Studies." *The School Musician* (May 1947), 18, no. 10, 32–33.

Green, Elizabeth A. H., "How Music Helps With Other Studies." *The Etude* (May 1947), 65, no. 5, 256, 286, 293.

Green, Elizabeth A. H., "Strings: The Strength of the Orchestra." *The School Musician* (June 1947), 18, no. 11, 30–31.

Green, Elizabeth A. H., "Strings: The Strength of the Orchestra." *The School Musician* (September 1947), 19, no. 2, 30–31.

Green, Elizabeth A. H., "Strings: The Strength of the Orchestra." *The School Musician* (October 1947), 19, no. 3, 30–31.

Green, Elizabeth A. H., "Strings: The Strength of the Orchestra." *The School Musician* (November 1947), 19, no. 4, 33–33.

Green, Elizabeth A. H., "Strings: The Strength of the Orchestra." *The School Musician* (January 1948), 19, no. 6, 30–31.

Green, Elizabeth A. H., "Strings: The Strength of the Orchestra." *The School Musician* (February 1948), 19, no. 7, 34–35.

Green, Elizabeth A. H., "Strings: The Strength of the Orchestra." *The School Musician* (April 1948), 19, no. 9, 34–35.

Green, Elizabeth A. H., "Strings: The Strength of the Orchestra." *The School Musician* (May 1948), 19, no. 10, 30–31.

Green, Elizabeth A. H., "Strings: The Strength of the Orchestra." *The School Musician* (October 1948), 20, no. 3, 32–33.

Green, Elizabeth A. H., "Strings: The Strength of the Orchestra." *The School Musician* (November 1948), 20, no. 4, 38–39.

Green, Elizabeth A. H., "Strings: The Strength of the Orchestra." *The School Musician* (December 1948), 20, no. 5, 38–39.

Green, Elizabeth A. H., "Strings: The Strength of the Orchestra." *The School Musician* (January 1949), 20, no. 6, 38–39.

Green, Elizabeth A. H., "Strings: The Strength of the Orchestra." *The School Musician* (February 1949), 20, no. 7, 32–33.

Green, Elizabeth A. H., "Strings: The Strength of the Orchestra." *The School Musician* (March 1949), 20, no. 8, 38–39.

Green, Elizabeth A. H., "Strings: The Strength of the Orchestra." *The School Musician* (April 1949), 20, no. 9, 34–35.

Green, Elizabeth A. H., "Strings: The Strength of the Orchestra." *The School Musician* (May 1949), 20, no. 10, 33.

Green, Elizabeth A. H., "Meadowmount." *American String Teacher* (January 1951), 1, no. 1.

Green, Elizabeth A. H., "Three Works I Would Hate to Teach Without." *Repertoire* (October 1951), 1, no. 1, 44–46.

Green, Elizabeth A. H., "The Student's First Violin Concerto." *Repertoire* (November 1951), 1, no. 2, 108–109.

Green, Elizabeth A. H., "Those Little 'Extra' Violin Books." *Repertoire* (January 1952), 1, no. 3, 166–168.

Green, Elizabeth A. H., "A Few Principles and Teachings of Ivan Galamian." *American String Teacher* (Spring 1956), 6, no. 2, 5, 8.

Green, Elizabeth A. H., "Twenty-Six Days in the Soviet Union." *American String Teacher* (January 1959), 9, no. 1, 1–2.

Green, Elizabeth A. H., "The Training of Conductors in the Soviet Union." *American String Teacher* (Spring 1960), 10, no. 2, 12.

Green, Elizabeth A. H., "Updating Conducting Technique." *The Instrumentalist* (April 1960), 14, no. 8, 34–35.

Green, Elizabeth A. H., "Violin Pedagogy." *American Music Teacher* (January–February 1961), 10, no. 3, 8, 19.

Green, Elizabeth A. H., "Violin Intonation and Muscular Development." *The Instrumentalist* (February 1961), 15, no. 6, 76–77.

Green, Elizabeth A. H., "On the Teaching of Conducting." *Music Educators Journal* (June–July 1961), 47, no. 6, 50, 55–56.

Green, Elizabeth A. H., "Conference Develops Ideas on Creative String Teaching." *American String Teacher* (November–December 1961), 11, no. 1, 21–22.

Green, Elizabeth A. H., "What Is Conducting Technique?" *Music Journal* (June–July 1961), 20, no. 1, 52–53, 90–91.

Green, Elizabeth A. H., "Let's Teach Our Students to Teach." *American Music Teacher* (January–February 1962), 11, no. 3, 10, 31.

Green, Elizabeth A. H., "Is Music Worth the Price?" *The Instrumentalist* (April 1962), 16, no. 8, 34–36.

Green, Elizabeth A. H., "Creativity in Performance." *Music Educators Journal* (November–December 1963), 50, no. 2, 69–70.

Green, Elizabeth A. H., "Wind Instruments in the Orchestra." *The Instrumentalist* (April 1964), 19, no. 2, 33–34, 69.

Green, Elizabeth A. H., "An Open Letter to All Conductors of Youth Orchestras" *American String Teacher* (Fall 1964), 14, no. 1, 13.

Green, Elizabeth A. H., "Band and Orchestra Conducting – Techniques and Musicianship." *The Instrumentalist* (April 1969), 23, no. 9, 51–52.

Green, Elizabeth A. H., "For a More Professional High School Orchestra." *The Instrumentalist* (May 1969), 23, no. 10, 66–67.

Green, Elizabeth A. H., and Potter, L. "A Progressive Course of Study of String Quartets." *American String Teacher* (Winter 1972), 22, no. 1, 30, 32.

Green, Elizabeth A. H., "Then and Now." *American String Teacher* (Spring 1977), 27, no. 2, 14.

Newspaper

Green, Elizabeth A. H., "Schools' Music Program Explained and Lauded." *Ann Arbor News* (May 16, 1957).

Book Publications

Green, Elizabeth A. H., *Orchestral Bowings and Routines* (1st ed.). Ann Arbor, MI: Ann Arbor Publishers, 1949.

Green, Elizabeth A. H., *First Steps in the Galamian Bowing Method*, 1950.

Green, Elizabeth A. H., *Orchestral Bowings and Routines* (2nd ed.). Ann Arbor, MI: Campus Pubs, 1957.

Green, Elizabeth A. H., *Hohman, for the String Class*. New York: Carl Fischer, 1959.

Green, Elizabeth A. H., *Theme and Variations*. New York: Carl Fischer, 1960.

Galamian, Ivan, *Principles of Violin Playing and Teaching*. Englewood Cliffs, New Jersey: Prentice-Hall, Inc., 1961.

Green, Elizabeth A. H., *The Modern Conductor* (1st ed.). Englewood Cliffs, New Jersey: Prentice-Hall, Inc., 1961.

Green, Elizabeth, A. H., *Musicianship and Repertoire for the High School Orchestra*. Bryn Mawr, Pennsylvania: Theodore Presser, 1962.

Green, Elizabeth A. H., *Teaching String Instruments in Classes*. Englewood Cliffs, New Jersey: Prentice-Hall, Inc., 1966.

Green, Elizabeth A. H., *Increasing the Proficiency on the Violin*. Philadelphia, Pennsylvania: Elkan-Vogel Co., 1967.

Green, Elizabeth A. H., *The Modern Conductor* (2nd ed.). Englewood Cliffs, New Jersey: Prentice-Hall, Inc., 1968.

Green, Elizabeth A. H., and Malko, Nicolai. *The Conductor and His Score* (1st ed.). Englewood Cliffs, New Jersey: Prentice-Hall, Inc., 1975.

Green, Elizabeth A. H., *The Modern Conductor* (3rd ed.). Englewood Cliffs, New Jersey: Prentice-Hall, Inc., 1981.

Green, Elizabeth A. H., and Malko, Nicolai. *The Conductor and His Score* (2nd ed.). Englewood Cliffs, New Jersey: Prentice-Hall, Inc., 1985.

Green, Elizabeth A. H., *The Modern Conductor* (4th ed.). Englewood Cliffs, New Jersey: Prentice-Hall, Inc., 1987.

Green, Elizabeth, A. H., *The Dynamic Orchestra.* Englewood Cliffs, New Jersey: Prentice-Hall, Inc., 1987.

Green, Elizabeth A. H., *Orchestral Bowings and Routines* (3rd ed.). Fairfax, VA: American String Teachers Association, 1990.

Green, Elizabeth A. H., *The Modern Conductor* (5th ed.). Englewood Cliffs, New Jersey: Prentice-Hall, Inc., 1992.

Green, Elizabeth A. H., *Miraculous Teacher: Ivan Galamian and the Meadowmount Experience.* Bryn Mawr, Pennsylvania: Theodore Presser, 1993.

Green, Elizabeth A. H., *The Modern Conductor* (6th ed.). Englewood Cliffs, New Jersey: Prentice-Hall, Inc., 1997.

Green, Elizabeth A. H., *The Modern Conductor* (7th ed.). Englewood Cliffs, New Jersey: Prentice-Hall, Inc., 2003.

Green, Elizabeth, A. H., *Practicing Successfully.* Chicago, Illinois: GIA Publications, 2006.

Appendix B
Selected Compositions

Green, Elizabeth A. H. *Minuet and Trio for String Quartet*, n.d.

Green, Elizabeth A. H. *Caprice de Concert, op. 1. (for violin with piano accompaniment)*, manuscript, circa 1926.

Green, Elizabeth A. H. *Les Airs Mysterieux (for violin with piano accompaniment)*, manuscript, circa 1926.

Green, Elizabeth A. H. *Largo (by Arcangelo Corelli, arrangement) (for 2 flutes, 1 oboe, 2 clarinets in A, 2 Bassoons, 2 horns in F)*, manuscript, July 15, 1938.

Green, Elizabeth A. H. *Chatterbox Symphonette*, manuscript, 1950.

Green, Elizabeth A. H. *Theme and Variations for Teaching Orchestral Bowings*, New York City, New York: Carl Fischer, 1960.

Green, Elizabeth A. H. *Twelve Modern Etudes for Advanced Violinists and Violists*, Philadelphia, Pennsylvania: Elkan-Vogel Company, 1964.

Green, Elizabeth A. H. *Fiddle Sessions* (with Livingston Gearhart), manuscript, 1967.

Green, Elizabeth A. H. *Sinfonia in D (by Karl Stamitz, arrangement)*, manuscript, 1970.

Appendix C
Awards

Michigan Federation of Music Clubs *Teacher of the Year Award*, 1967.

Membership in Wheaton College's *Scholastic Honor Society*, 1974.

Distinguished Service Award from American String Teachers Association, 1976.

Distinguished Career Award from Northwestern University Alumni Association, 1978.

Golden Rose Award, Women Band Directors National Association, 1982.

Outstanding Service to Music, Tau Beta Sigma, 1986.

Honorary Membership, Phi Beta Mu, 1986.

Medal of Honor, Midwest International Band and Orchestra Clinic, 1988.

Honorary Membership, University of Michigan Band, 1988.

Allen Britton nominated Honorary Doctorate Eastern Michigan University, 1991.

Edwin Franko Goldman Memorial Citation, American Bandmasters Association, 1992.

Michigan House of Representatives Resolution, 1995.

National Honorary Member, Delta Omicron Music Fraternity.

Appendix D
Methodology

The significance of this project for some readers resides in the stories of Elizabeth A. H. Green's musical teaching itself – the "what." Alternatively, the significance of this project for other readers lies in the design serving as a model for studying the lives and contributions of other music educators. This appendix is intended for the latter audience.

Methodological Overview

Historical researchers use a myriad of investigative tools to study people and events within the field of education, and no single investigative tool can provide a complete illustration of this complex purpose. Furthermore, there appears to be a need to document remarkable music educators and learn from their wealth of experiences – both successes and setbacks. Within this study, I incorporated elements of both life history and oral history research designs.

Life History

The purpose of life history inquiry is to gain insights into the broader human condition through knowing and understanding the experiences of other humans. Historical researchers who utilize life history research design recognize that the individual, or subject of inquiry, is a window into broader social and societal conditions.[1] Through applying the purpose and definition of life history inquiry to this study, the memories of and artifacts associated with Green serve as windows into the complexity of instrumental music and conducting pedagogy, as well as the nuance and role of a teacher's relational capacity in music teaching and learning.

Life history research relies on and depicts the storied nature of lives while honoring the individuality and complexity of individuals' experiences.[2] However, life history research also extends beyond the individuals and frames their narrative accounts and interpretations within the broader context and phenomenon of interest.[3] A few emblematic characteristics of a life history research project include: (1) a few participants or informants whom the researcher studies in substantial depth; (2) the researcher gathering data over an extended period of time using techniques such as interviewing, participant observation, and artifact collection; (3) coding these data and connecting themes to discipline-based theories; and (4) presenting these data in detailed life history accounts.[4]

Researchers in music have studied the lives of individuals using life history research designs, and life stories exist for music education topics related to music student teaching[5] and beginning music teachers.[6] Fewer researchers have specifically examined instrumental music teachers using a life history approach.[7] Given the few life histories examining topics in music education and the complexity of instrumental music and conducting pedagogy, life history inquiry can provide new information not yet already uncovered. Moreover, McCarthy demonstrates that "the writing and publication of life stories of music teachers would be most valuable for the profession ... those of retired teachers can be of special significance."[8]

Oral History

Another research method utilized by historical researchers is gathering participant oral histories through interviews, and this method has become progressively popular over the last decade.[9] Simply put, oral history is a method of historical documentation that allows the researcher to participate in creating the historical document.[10] Etter-Lewis states that oral history

> preserves an individual's own words and perspectives in a particularly authentic way. It is a collaborative transaction that reconstructs a life once lived; and it is a text that makes relevant to the present metaphors of a narrator's past. ... The spontaneity of oral history reveals a virtually unedited and sometimes unprocessed view of personal meaning and judgment that is note altered by the usual limitations of written language.[11]

I utilized oral history to accomplish the purpose of this research. The purpose of oral history is to document memories and reflections of past events as seen by a single or multiple research participant(s). Oral history differs from autobiographical research, as the interaction between the researcher and informant during a semi-structured interview assists in stimulating memories.[12] Moreover, oral history is a method of historical documentation that allows the researcher to participate in creating the historical document.[13]

Oral and Life Histories Combined

In order to understand the complexity of instrumental music and conducting pedagogy, I needed to combine elements of both oral and life history inquiry. Both oral history and life history inquiry are exasperatingly imprecise terms, and their definitions are as many as their uses. Given the previous definitions and purposes, I combined elements of both life and oral history inquiry into a hybrid research design to accomplish the purpose of this study. Before I describe the combination of methodological elements, I maintain that informant interview data are components of both research methods and this element was crucial to completing my purpose. In order to accomplish the purpose of the study, I argue that a hallmark of the oral history method, the interaction between the researcher and informant during a semi-structured interview, assisted in stimulating memories to include within the narrative accounts.[14] This process allowed me to participate in creating the historical document.[15] Consequently, I preserved the element of life history research that frames an informant's narrative accounts and interpretations within the broader context and phenomenon of interest within this study.

Researcher Reflexivity

The method *life history* recognizes not only that personal, temporal, social, and contextual influences facilitate understanding of lives and phenomena being explored, but also that, from conceptualization through to representation of new understandings to others, any research project is an expression of elements of a researcher's life history.[16] As many historical researchers recommend, reflexivity is a crucial component to demonstrating trustworthiness, as researcher objectivity in the study of human lives is not possible. Schwalbe observes that "it could be that all my studies of other people are partly a roundabout way to know myself better."[17] It seems that the relational and situational qualities of our work as researchers is of prime importance in considering our own reflexivity.

In their book, *Qualitative Research: A Guide to Design and Implementation,* Merriam and Tisdell suggested that researchers explore their assumptions, biases, and relationship to the study.[18] I have a keen interest in string instrument and conducting pedagogy, and while reflexivity is an essential process, I cannot dismiss my own positionality. Positionality is defined in music education research as how one is situated within a social context as either privileged or disadvantaged.[19] As a former secondary school instrumental music educator and doctoral student in music education at the University of Michigan, I was aware of Elizabeth Green's legacy, teachings, and positive impact on string instrument and conducting pedagogy in the Great Lakes region of the United States and beyond. My music teacher preparation program used her conducting textbook, *The Modern Conductor,*[20] and I enrolled in additional coursework focused on large music ensemble pedagogy and applied conducting. These experiences helped shape my own understanding of how Green's life and career in music education became an important component of stringed-instrument and conducting pedagogy.

Research Setting and Data Sources

Considering the place and space of conducting research offers insights into the social and cultural contexts. In his book, *Musicking: The Meanings of Performing and Listening,* Small stated that a physical space can influence a human's social behaviors, specifically when considering the role of performance venues in framing how human's experience music.[21] Furthermore, the role of a research context or setting is essential to understanding life history and oral history inquiry. Therefore, framing data generated from this study requires an explanation of the research setting and informant selection process. In this section of the appendix, I first describe the research setting – "the where." Following the description of the research setting, I then describe how informants were selected and how they interacted with or are connected to Green.

Research Setting

The majority of the research and data collection was conducted on the campus of Green's final position in higher education, the University of Michigan. Preliminary investigation of Green's life and career in music education began in March 2014 by scanning and reading the Elizabeth A. H. Green Papers housed within the Bentley Historical Library on the campus of the University of Michigan. After I finished my first year as a music education faculty member at the University of Utah, I reviewed my notes about Green's collection of papers and explored options of interviewing her former students, faculty colleagues, and friends. Next, I returned to the University of Michigan campus and scheduled in-person interviews with informants during September and October of 2017. Additionally, I studied the contents of the Elizabeth A. H. Green Papers housed within the Bentley Historical Library when I was not interviewing informants. Over the calendar year, I scheduled interviews with almost two dozen informants on computer-mediated platforms (e.g., Zoom, Skype). Information about the criteria for selection appears within the next section of this appendix. After transcribing the interview transcripts and outlining Green's biographical information, a few discrepancies around Green's employment record surfaced. My final trip Bentley Historical Library involved consulting the university's human resource records and additional School of Music, Theatre, and Dance documents.

Data Sources

There are two categories of sources from which historical evidence is gathered – primary and secondary sources. For historical researchers, primary sources are "the gold standard of historical research."[22] I reviewed multiple volumes of the *Journal of Historical Research in Music Education* and found that McCarthy reported a variety of primary sources utilized in historical investigations.[23] Primary sources are delineated into three broad categories, including written documents (e.g., journal entries, correspondence, newspaper articles, magazine articles, quantitative records, meeting notes), oral records (e.g., interviews, audio and visual recordings), and artifacts (e.g., instructional materials, photographs, textbooks).[24]

Written Documents

A variety of written documents were consulted during this study. There are two collections of materials titled the Elizabeth Green Papers. One is located at the University of Michigan and served as a primary archive of evidence. The other collection of Elizabeth Green Papers is housed at Wheaton College and served as an archive to confirm evidence. These papers highlight the activities of Green, a music educator and performer, and include biographical material, published articles, business and personal correspondence, music education materials, memorabilia, monographs, performance programs, personal journals, and lectures. Several written documents within both collections of the Elizabeth Green Papers that are germane to the current study include published newspaper and magazine articles, as well as correspondence from music teachers, her former students, and her conducting teacher, Nicoli Malko. A second source of written documentation was university records associated with Elizabeth Green, including human resource and personnel files, the School of Music, Theatre, and Dance executive committee meeting minutes, and press releases. A third source of written documentation that I consulted was an unpublished dissertation including a biographical information about Elizabeth Green between the years 1906 and 1974.[25] The final source of written documentation was my reflexive journal. Journal writing as a reflexive research activity is called "reflexive journaling," and many qualitative researchers advocate the use of a reflexive journal at multiple points in the research project timeline.[26] The reflexive journal is one approach to documenting how a study was designed and what techniques were selected, as well as for tracking potential ethical issues involved in the study.

Oral Records

Prior to conducting this study, few oral records existed about Elizabeth Green. In the Elizabeth Green Papers (University of Michigan) were an audio recording of her 1978 guest lecture at the University of Connecticut and an audio recording of her teaching a conducting class (date unknown). During the planning stages of this investigation, video footage of Elizabeth Green conducting at the SSA Conducting Competition in 1980 was published.[27] Additionally, video footage of Elizabeth Green demonstrating Malko's conducting exercises, as written in *The Modern Conductor*,[28] was published.[29] Given these limited oral records, I conducted life and oral history interviews with Green's former students, faculty colleagues, and friends. Details about the interviews appear later within this appendix.

Artifacts

Within the Elizabeth Green Papers, there are dozens of photographs of Green throughout her teaching career. Several paper artifacts germane to the current study exist in the archive and include: course syllabi, conducting course examinations, conducting clinic lecture notes, and non-published writings on stringed instrument and conducting pedagogy. These artifacts were essential to this study for two reasons. First, the artifacts informed the creation of a detailed interview protocol.

Second, the artifacts and oral records were used to stimulate memories of pedagogy/classroom practice.

Informant Selection and Interviews

Historians assert that understanding the past can be expanded by locating and obtaining insights into why events may have happened and who may have played a role in these past events.[30] Given the purpose of this study, I located primary sources as well as people who witnessed Elizabeth Green teach stringed instruments and conducting to provide firsthand evidence about her life and career in music education. As the primary approach to documenting the life and career of Elizabeth Green, I chose interviewing informants as a data collection strategy.

Informant Selection

Selecting informants to accomplish the purpose of this study was a demanding task. As with archival research, the collection of data from interviews requires prior knowledge about the specific kind of information needed to answer the research questions. Informants were identified using a two-stage stratified purposeful sampling protocol.[31] The first stage of selecting informants involved developing a pool of possible informants through informal conversations with current music faculty at the University of Michigan. Faculty were selected as the first stage because I have a strong rapport with former mentors and teachers, with two emeritus faculty members having had previous professional relationships with Elizabeth Green.

During the second stage, I had an informal conversation with one informant to help identify additional informants. Michael Patton explains that network sampling is a "strategy in which a small number of initial participants from the target population ('seeds') are studied and asked to recruit … hard-to-access participants."[32] A pool of 24 potential informants was developed from this stage of sampling, and I invited all to participate. Of the 24 possible informants, six did not respond to my attempts to make contact by phone or email communication. Four informants initially responded to my invitation and later withdrew from the study, and 14 responded, consented to, and participated in the interview process. Based on the interview data, I categorized the informants into two categories: primary and secondary. Primary informants are former students and colleagues who have had extended relationships with Green, while secondary informants may have only had Green for one or two classes. Hesse-Biber and Leavy state that "oral history is a special method of interview where the researcher and research participants spend extended time together engaged in a process of storytelling and listening. In other words, oral history is a collaborative process of narrative building."[33]

Interview Protocol

Interviewing is an ancient technique, defined by Janesick as "a meeting of two persons to exchange information and ideas through questions and responses, resulting in communication and joint construction of meaning about a particular topic."[34] A semi-structured interview protocol was designed around the existing artifacts and collated with the research questions. Questions were worded by chronology (first this, then this) and causality (this → this).

Before the interviews, I asked an established and well-known music education historian to review my interview protocol as a validation strategy. She provided feedback on the protocol, which included restructuring two questions to include experience/example and comparison/contrast components.[35] I sent the interview questions approximately one week prior to the agreed upon date and time and confirmed details about the meeting place for all in-person interviews. Most of the interviews were requested and conducted by phone or computer-mediated communication (CMC), including Skype or other similar technologies, and study procedures for this investigation were approved by the Institutional Review Board at the University of Utah (IRB_00097311; Exemption Date: November 14, 2016).

During the interviews, all conversations were audio recorded using a Zoom H4N PRO Digital Multitrack Recorder and video recorded (when in-person) using a Canon VIXIA HF R700 Full HD Camcorder. Three in-person interviews were conducted in a variety of locations in Ann Arbor, Michigan, including one interview on the campus of the University of Michigan. At two moments during the interviews, I used voice recordings of Green to stimulate conversation and elicit meaning about her pedagogy. This interdisciplinary approach is a borrowed technique associated with stimulated recall and elicitation.[36]

Informed consent was requested of all informants in writing and verbally during the interviews. One of the most persistent questions for historical researchers has to do with identifying informants.[37] On one hand, documenting someone's life requires knowing who the informant is. On the other hand, certain sensitive situations may require pseudonyms. This ethical issue concerns confidentiality and anonymity. To protect the informants in this study, each was interviewed separately and their identities have been withheld. This protocol is commonplace in historical research; however, some historical researchers do not protect the identity of their informants. Most oral history interviewing projects are not subject to the requirements of Department of Health and Human Services (HHS) regulations for the protections of human subjects[38] and can be excluded from IRB oversight. This study was excluded from oversight. Informant interviews ranged in length from 60 to 90 minutes.

Establishing rapport with informants was a complex process, and my aim was to develop trust and respect so that a robust account of past events was possible. Seidman discusses how rapport is a balance between interviewer and the interviewed and suggests that "the interviewing relationship must be marked by respect, interest, attention, and good manners on the part of the interviewer."[39] Therefore, rapport was a necessary component of the interview strategy. I established rapport with informants by using four strategies: (1) communicating my intention with the study and acknowledging what specific contributions the informant's memories could make; (2) welcoming the informant and priming them for the interview by asking them questions about their current and past experiences with stringed instruments and/ or conducting (for in-person interviews, I would subtly mirror the informant's body language or intentionally reposition myself in a neutral sitting position); (3) listening to details divulged by the informants and occasionally repeating some of their comments back to them as a variation of member checking strategies; and (4) always providing opportunities to ask questions during the semi-structured interview.

After the interviews, transcripts of the interviews were generated and the informants were asked to confirm their words prior to analysis. Additional protections of informant transcripts included the closure of defamatory material and avoiding stereotypes and misrepresentation or manipulations of the informant's words.

Data Verification, Collective Interpretation, and Analysis

Despite these emblematic characteristics of life history and oral history inquiry, there is no set of techniques or formulae for data verification and analysis. Within this section of the appendix, I explain my strategies for verifying, interpreting, and analyzing these data.

Data Verification

Reporting the strategies for data verification is crucial to all historical investigations. Otherwise, the quality of research cannot be assessed and the veracity of the research is in question. As a way of criticizing the primary sources, McCarthy suggests that each source be subjected to external and internal criticism.[40] I followed McCarthy's suggestions and data verification protocol.

During the verification process, there were occasional instances of conflicting data. One example of conflicting data was Elizabeth Green's birthdate. Her birthdate has been verified through several sources, including a self-endorsed biography, and is documented as August 21, 1906. However, in two primary sources, a University of Michigan-produced biography from 1960 and budget information prepared in 1950, the authors wrote Green's birthdate as August 22, 1906. Establishing the authenticity and reliability of her birthdate was essential to this study, and given the breadth of primary sources documenting the first date, it is clear that an error was made from this 1960 document. Another example of conflicting data resides in the memories of her former students and colleagues. Memories are complex, and given the protracted time away from Green, establishing the accuracy and credibility of memories required an additional layer of scrutiny. For some informants, prompting them using audio of Green's voice may have triggered memories and stories that might otherwise have been difficult to describe or remember without using the audio prompt. While dozens of memories about Green's teaching were positive and laudable, two informants presented diverging evidence, and this caused intense reflection on my part. I sought to understand the motivation of the informant, their experiences with Green, and when these experiences occurred during her life and career. Despite the process of verifying, the primary sources revealed an occasional discrepancy among these data; however, these instances were few.

Collective Interpretation and Analysis

In his book *Documents of Life: An Introduction to the Problems and Literature of a Humanistic Method*, Plummer describes the data analysis process of life history data:

> In many ways this is the truly creative part of the work. It entails brooding and reflecting upon mounds of data for long periods of time until it "makes sense" and "feels right," and key ideas and themes flow from it. It is also the hardest process to describe: the standard technique is to read and make notes, leave and ponder, reread without notes, make new notes, match notes up, ponder, reread, and so on.[41]

Transcripts were made of all interview data sets, and to ensure accuracy, informants had an opportunity to verify their thoughts, opinions, and observations. These transcripts were verbatim from the interviews.

Data analysis included several protocols for assuring triangulation, trustworthiness, and transferability.[42] One component of trustworthiness was the use of member checks. Member checks allowed the informants the opportunity to rephrase and rearticulate their thoughts, should they feel differently about what was initially stated. Throughout the interview process, I used clarifying questions to confirm the details of the interviews. A second component of trustworthiness for this study was data saturation. Data saturation in historical research is important to the content validity of an investigation.[43] The last component contributing to trustworthiness in this oral history was researcher–interviewee rapport.

My approach to inspecting the interview data occurred in two simultaneous stages. The first stage involved locating two qualified external reviewers to independently inspect the interview data (each external reviewer was masked to the other external reviewer). To minimize potential bias, each external reviewer had prior qualitative research experience and were employed as instrumental music teacher educators. Each external reviewer volunteered to independently check the transcripts, and I trained both reviewers on the coding procedures prior to analysis. The second simultaneous stage involved my transcript coding. First, I began relistening to each interview and taking notes in my reflexive journal. Next, I visited the transcripts of these interviews and utilized an open-ended coding procedure while examining these data. Then, I used inductive analysis to compare, sort, and synthesize these data. Lastly, I used axial coding to group like codes into larger themes. Following both stages of analysis, I interviewed the external reviewers to discuss coding discrepancies until we reached consensus.

While interpreting oral history narratives means examining for underlying patterns of meaning within the interview, within this context, sometimes meaning can be construed from what is not said.[44] Once themes were identified from the interview transcripts, I proceeded to examine the archive to corroborate or contradict these themes from written documents and artifacts related to her pedagogy. The analysis process of uncovering the complexities from these data sources was challenging, and it was the longest stage in this investigation. Analysis is a process of listening closely.

The process of revisiting the data multiple times illuminated nuances in the interviewee's thinking, disposition, and implicit bias over the course of the interviews. The process of revisiting the data multiple times provided me with an opportunity to understand the interviewee's experience from their point of view, including developing an understanding of their life experiences in a detailed way. Through reading and re-reading the interview transcripts, listening deeply to their interview responses, and watching their non-verbal cues on campus and in the middle school, I developed a capacity to interpret how the participants made sense of their life experiences and their experiences with Elizabeth. The findings described within the chapters emerged from an extensive research process of discovery that centered on a detailed study of the life and career of Elizabeth A. H. Green.

Notes

1 Ardra L. Cole and J. Gary Knowles, "What is Life History Research," in *Lives in Context: The Art of Life History Research*, eds. Ardra L. Cole and J. Gary Knowles (Lanham, MD: Alta Mira Press, 2001), 12.

2 Cole and Knowles, 20.

3 Ibid.

4 Cole and Knowles, 13.

5 M. E. Schmidt, "Learning From Experiences: Influences on Music Teachers' Perceptions and Practices," Ph.D. diss., University of Michigan, Ann Arbor, 1994, ProQuest Dissertations and Theses Global (UMI No. 9423310).

6 D. C. Baker, "Music Service Teachers' Life Histories in the United Kingdom With Implications for Practice," *International Journal of Music Education* 23, no. 3 (2005): 251–266; D. C. Baker, "Life Histories of Music Service Teachers: The Past in Inductee's Present," *British Journal of Music Education* 23, no. 1 (2006): 39–50; M. Schmidt and J. G. Knowles, "'Why Don't They Listen to Me?': Cooperating Teachers' and Supervisors' Advice to Music Student Teachers," paper presented at the annual meeting of the Association of Teacher Educators (February 1994), Atlanta, Georgia; Schmidt and Knowles, "Four Women's Stories of Failure as Beginning Teachers," *Teaching & Teacher Education* 11, no. 5 (1995): 429–444.

7 C. Morgan, "Instrumental Music Teaching and Learning: A Life History Approach," Ph.D. diss., University of Exeter, United Kingdom, 1998, ProQuest Dissertations and Theses Global (UMI No. U109390).

8 Marie McCarthy, "Narrative Inquiry as a Way of Knowing in Music Education," *Research Studies in Music Education* 29, no. 1 (2007): 3–12; 8

9 Gary McCulloch and William Richardson, *Historical Research in Educational Settings* (Philadelphia: Open University Press, 2000), 113.

10 George N. Heller and Bruce D. Wilson, "Historical Research," in *The Handbook of Research on Music Teaching and Learning*, ed. Richard Colwell (New York: Schirmer Books, 1992), 102.

11 G. Etter-Lewis, *My Soul Is My Own: Oral Narratives of African American Women in the Professions* (New York: Routledge, 1993), xii.

12 Barbara Sommer and Mary Kay Quinlan, *The Oral History Manual* (New York: Alta Mira Press, 2002), 1.

13 Heller and Wilson, 102.

14 Sommer and Quinlan, 1.

15 Heller and Wilson, 102.

16 Cole and Knowles, 10.

17 M. Schwalbe, "The Work of Professing (A Letter to Home)," in *This Fine Place So Far From Home: Voices of Academics From the Working Class*, eds. C. L. Barney Dews and C. Leste Law (Philadelphia: Temple University Press, 1995), 331.

18 Sharan B. Merriam and Elizabeth J. Tisdell, *Qualitative Research: A Guide to Design and Implementation*, 4th ed. (New York: John Wiley & Sons, 2016).

19 Nicole R. Robinson, "Developing a Critical Consciousness for Diversity and Equity Among Preservice Music Teachers," *Journal of Music Teacher Education* 26, no. 3 (2017): 12.

20 Elizabeth A. Green, *The Modern Conductor: A College Text Based on the Technical Principles of Nicolai Malko as Set Forth in His 'The Conductor and His Baton* (Upper Saddle River, NJ: Prentice-Hall, 1997).

21 Christopher Small, *Musicking: The Meanings of Performing and Listening* (Middletown, CT: Wesleyan University Press, 1998).

22 E. A. Danto, *Historical Research* (Oxford: Oxford University Press, 2008), 62.

23 Marie McCarthy, "A Content Analysis of Articles Published in Volumes 21–30 of the *Journal of Historical Research in Music Education*: Assessing Developments and Trends in Historical Research," paper presented at the Chattanooga Symposium on the History of Music Education. Chattanooga, TN, June 2–4, 2011.

24 Marie McCarthy, "Historical Inquiry: Inside the Process," in *Inquiry in Music Education: Concepts and Methods for the Beginning Researcher*, eds. Hildegard Froehlich and Carol Frierson-Campbell (New York: Routledge, 2013), 133.

25 Deborah Annette Smith, "Elizabeth A. H. Green: A Biography," Ph.D. diss., University of Michigan, Ann Arbor, 1986, ProQuest Dissertations and Theses Global (UMI No. 8621380)

26 Valerie J. Janesick, *Oral History for the Qualitative Researcher: Choreographing the Story* (New York: Guilford Press, 2010), 107.

27 Elizabeth A. Green, "SSA Conducting Competition 1980," *YouTube*, 22:35, February 12, 2016, www.youtube.com/watch?v=LSKYlqq1RnM.

28 Green, *Modern Conductor*.

29 Elizabeth A. Green, "Malko Conducting Exercises," *YouTube*, 25:57, February 8, 2017, www.youtube.com/watch?v=oZYFi89Ph4g.

30 Edward L. Rainbow and Hildegard C. Froehlich, *Research in Music Education: An Introduction to Systematic Inquiry* (New York: Schirmer Books, 1987), 107.

31 Michael Quinn Patton, *Qualitative Research & Evaluation Methods: Integrating Theory and Practice* (Thousand Oaks, CA: Sage, 2014), 435.

32 Patton, 299.
33 Sharlene Nagy Hesse-Biber and Patricia Leavy, *The Practice of Qualitative Research* (Sage, 2011), 152.
34   Janesick, 46.
35 Janesick, 47.
36 Anna Harris, "Eliciting Sound Memories," *The Public Historian* 37, no. 4 (2015): 15.
37 Janesick, 52.
38 Janesick, 225.
39 Irving Seidman, *Interviewing as Qualitative Research: A Guide for Researchers in Education and the Social Sciences*, 3rd ed. (New York: Teachers college Press, 2006), 97.
40 McCarthy, "Historical Inquiry," 135–137.
41 K. Plummer, *Documents of Life: An Introduction to the Problems and Literature of a Humanistic Model* (London: George Allen & Unwin, 1983), 99.
42 Patton, 435.
43 Patricia I. Fusch and Lawrence R. Ness, "Are We There Yet? Data Saturation in Qualitative Research," *The Qualitative Report* 20, no. 9 (2015): 1408–1416.
44 Linda Shopes, "Oral History," in *The SAGE Handbook of Qualitative Research*, ed. Norman Denzin and Yovanna Lincoln (Thousand Oaks, CA: Sage, 2011), 452.

Appendix E
Obituary

EDITH STAFF EMBREY, 88, a founding member of the Pleasant Ridge Club and resident of Royal Oak, died Thursday of natural causes at Palms of Pasadena Hospital in St. Petersburg, Fla.

Mrs. Embrey was a founding member of Shrine of the Little Flower parish in 1926. She served in the Civil Defense Corps during World War II, teaching first aid.

Her father, the late Charles Staff, was the first president of the Village of Pleasant Ridge in 1919, before its incorporation in 1928.

An avid golfer until recently, she was a lifelong member of Red Run Golf Club in Royal Oak.

Mrs. Embrey is survived by her son, Lee; three daughters, Janice McCarthy, Joan Labine and Sally Smith; a brother, 16 grandchildren and 21 great-grandchildren.

The funeral service is at 10 a.m. today at Shrine of the Little Flower Roman Catholic Church, 12 Mile and Woodward in Royal Oak. Burial will follow in Holy Sepulchre Cemetery in Southfield.

ELIZABETH A.H. GREEN, 89, an internationally known music instructor, died Sunday of cancer at her home in Ann Arbor.

An author of several instructional music publications, Miss Green began playing the violin at age 3½. She earned a bachelor's degree from Wheaton (Ill.) College in 1928 and her master's in music in 1939 from Northwestern University.

In 1942, she was appointed assistant professor of music education at the University of Michigan. She was concertmaster of the Ann Arbor Symphony Orchestra from 1942-62.

She retired from U-M in 1975 as professor emeritus. She later studied painting at Eastern Michigan University, earning a bachelor's in 1978.

She is survived by her cousin, Rebecca Ericsson Hunter.

Visitation will be 7-9 p.m. today at Muehlig Funeral Chapel, 403 S. Fourth Ave., Ann Arbor. A memorial service will be 4 p.m. Wednesday at First Presbyterian Church, 1432 Washtenaw Ave., Ann Arbor.

ANNE W. WRIGHT, 56, an art and antiques collector, died Saturday of a stroke at William Beaumont Hospital in Royal Oak. She was a longtime resident of Franklin.

A graduate of Cranbrook-Kings-

Index

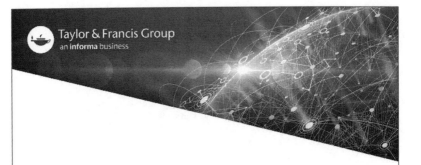

For Product Safety Concerns and Information please contact our EU
representative GPSR@taylorandfrancis.com Taylor & Francis Verlag GmbH,
Kaufingerstraße 24, 80331 München, Germany

Printed and bound by CPI Group (UK) Ltd, Croydon, CR0 4YY

11/04/2025

01844010-0016